WHAT IS CHRISTIAN LIFE?

IS VOLUME

56

OF THE

Twentieth Century Encyclopedia of Catholicism

·UNDER SECTION

V

THE LIFE OF FAITH

IT IS ALSO THE

78TH

VOLUME IN ORDER OF PUBLICATION

Edited by HENRI DANIEL-ROPS *of the Académie Française*

WHAT IS CHRISTIAN LIFE?

By P. A. LIÉGÉ, O.P.

Translated from the French by A. Manson

ꜱ

HAWTHORN BOOKS · PUBLISHERS · *New York*

First Edition, November, 1961

NIHIL OBSTAT

Joannes M. T. Barton, S.T.D., L.S.S.

   Censor Deputatus

IMPRIMATUR

E. Morrogh Bernard

   Vicarius Generalis

Westmonasterii, die XIX SEPTEMBRIS MCMLXI

CONTENTS

CHAPTER I

THE GOAL OF CHRISTIAN LIVING

The title of this book will doubtless lead readers to expect to discover herein an ideal of life, its justifying principles, its hopes and duties and its rules of conduct. In other words, an ethic, that ethic which many, even non-Christians, admire, and regard as the loftiest of human ideals. But to take this line would come nowhere near what is essential and original in Christian life. For that is something very different from an ideal and something more than a morality.

THE SOURCES OF CHRISTIAN LIFE

There is the fact of Jesus Christ. There are the events of Easter and Pentecost. From these arose a movement of life and spiritual renewal, a revolutionary universe within the order of human existence. The Christian movement: a before and after in the story of the deep issues of mankind. A decisive step upwards, a leap towards infinity from the world of human lives.

To become a Christian is to enter into this movement with every human potentiality, to allow its indwelling, to be directed by its energy, to be subject to its dynamism. And, after that, life is not what it was before. For this movement is a divine creation, God's bringing about of his ultimate purpose, already in view when he first created.

At any rate, that was how the first Christians looked at things. Jesus, that Master whose name they bore, was not merely the author of a better ideal, but the living principle of a universe reconciled and kneaded into shape by a divine power that surpassed it. God had come among men to give them a future and to give ballast to human affairs. The events of Easter and Pentecost, of which they were the witnesses, opened up for ever and for all men that divine adventure of advancement and growth first lived by Jesus. Most certainly every man must freely consent to answer God's call and to enter into the movement of Christian grace. But that movement was in existence before the initiative of each of those who became Christians. Most certainly it was not a miracle transforming existence on the spot, but a fundamental renewal carrying with it a solid hope. And Christians as a whole became aware of a new mankind, straining towards a future above and beyond the present.

Their life bore witness to this in the midst of a world still ignorant of the great deeds of God in history. The following extract from Peter's first letter to the newly baptized brings us an echo of it:

> Blessed be that God, that Father of our Lord Jesus Christ, who in his great mercy has begotten us anew, making hope live in us through the resurrection of Jesus Christ from the dead. We are to share an inheritance that is incorruptible, inviolable, unfading. It is stored up for you in heaven; and meanwhile through your faith, the power of God affords you safe conduct till you reach it, this salvation which is waiting to be disclosed at the end of time. Then you will be triumphant. What if you have trials of many sorts to sadden your hearts in this brief interval? That must needs happen, so that you may give proof of your faith, a much more precious thing than the gold we test by fire; proof which will bring you praise and glory, and honour when Jesus Christ is revealed. You never saw him, but you learned to love him; you may not see him even now, but you believe in him; and, if you continue to believe in him, how you will triumph! How ineffable your

joy will be, and how sublime, when you reap the fruit of that faith of yours, the salvation of your souls. (1 Peter 1. 2–10.)

From the beginning of Christianity the movement is continuous. It made no spectacular splash; it attempted no miraculous compulsion to human allegiance. At times it might even seem to have been held up by the false witness of those who use its name but do not live from it. But Christian grace continues its action in history; it is evidenced by those whom Jesus Christ gathers into one single life that transcends generations, races and civilizations. It is these who must be questioned if we would know what it is to live as a Christian.

THE ADVENTURE OF HOLINESS

The complete answer has already been given for us. To live as a Christian is to put one's existence into the ownership of Christian grace, so that it may be vivified by it; it is to enter into the universe of God's holiness which is the fulfilment of creation. To speak of holiness as designating Christian life is to risk being misunderstood, even by certain Christians. Still Bernanos was right when he wrote: "Holiness is an adventure, even the only adventure. Whoever has once understood this has entered the sanctuary of the Catholic faith, has felt within his mortal body the trembling of a dread different from that of death: a superhuman hope." More often than not we are strangely mistaken about sanctity. So, before trying to reach its secret, it is as well to begin by indicating the misconceptions about it.

It will be agreed that the saint often appears to be someone wholly exceptional. First, because he is rare, as rare as genius. An extraordinary vocation to which we of lesser talent are forbidden by modesty to aspire. Secondly, from the fact that he becomes known by deeds done at the peak of an incomparable life, while we belong to humdrum daily life without visions, revelations, ecstasies or stigmata. Lastly, because a saint seems to be born such. He hardly appears to have known resistance to evil, the conflict of doubt, the temptation of mere earthly happiness.

It is true that many lives of the saints, not shy of legend, confirm this conviction. The saints were admirable men, no doubt, but scarcely imitable, especially in the world of today. Such biographies can be put aside. When we speak of saints we naturally refer to those who are canonized. For the Church has chosen for us brethren who can be models, those who have a more typical, radiant and fulfilled holiness. But this does not leave us free to conclude that sanctity is a specialist's career. We are all called to be saints. Listen to the apostle Peter: "It is a holy God who has called you and you too must be holy in all the ordering of your lives. You must be holy, the Scripture says, because I am holy" (1 Peter 1. 5). And Paul: "God . . . has chosen us out, in Christ, before the foundation of the world, to be saints, to be blameless in his sight for love of him, marking us out beforehand (so his will decreed) to be his adopted children through Jesus Christ. Thus he would manifest the splendour of that grace by which he has taken us into his favour in the person of his beloved son" (Ephes. 1. 4–7). Faith contains the seed of that calling to holiness which is common to every believer. The canonized saints are there as a reminder of that call, which they fulfilled in an exceptional way, but in no sense to dispense us from fulfilling it ourselves.

We can visit the places where the saints have lived and see how they shared in human social life. But we ought also to observe how out of these quite ordinary men God made, with their consent, those beings who bring the divine presence and power before us with compelling certitude. God has acted with power and man has given a proper response. We become holy, we are not born holy, and life is given us precisely to become holy, to shape our eternal destiny in cooperation with God. For a baptized person never to have wished to become a saint would be a serious matter.

For it would be a grave misunderstanding of holiness to

see it merely as moral perfection, with man as its sole architect, and God just occasionally lending a helping hand in
difficulties. To have no defects, to have overcome the instincts
and passions is not yet holiness. Holiness is a divine adventure
to which man is invited by God himself. The saint must not
be confused with the voluntarist ascetic or the hysterical
fanatic. Nor is he simply a man of honour, a social reformer
or a sage.

In any case, the saints do not hide their secret: Jesus Christ
lives again in them, adding their lives to his. In their life the
Gospel comes to life again: they are men of the Gospel.
Divine vitality and energy is transferred from Jesus Christ
to them, and in them the grace of Christian revelation is
active. Why not to the same extent in us?

CHAPTER II

CHRISTIAN EXISTENCE ON TRIAL

To non-Christians the meaning of Christian life is usually understood as that conception of human existence and moral behaviour which finds expression in the generality of the baptized.

At the present time, in a number of forms, in plays, philosophical essays and films, we encounter systems justifying a way of life totally opposed to what is considered to be Christian morality. Two major accusations stand out: firstly, that the Christian code defies life, and secondly that the Christian code defies history. What have we left if life and history are taken from us? However, we can hear what they have to say.

THE CHRISTIAN CODE DEFIES LIFE

Your morality, they tell us, defies life. First, because it forms a code of behaviour that is pre-existent to the concrete man that I am. It is not concerned with incorporating itself into the vital impulse within me, into the real development of my personality, my search for coherence and joy amid the daily elements of my destiny. It is an artificial morality and, in spite of your assertions, it lacks spiritual vigour, the tragic sense and a disinterested esteem for the human person, and also because without possibility of discussion it forbids me to totalize my human experience, to yield to the spontaneity of universal life calling multifariously within me.

In this appeal to life we recognize the loftiest spiritual demand of the non-Christian humanisms of our time, that instinct of a man conscious of himself and of his creative freedom, that sense of personal destiny involved in each day's activities. Freedom, spontaneity, commitment, destiny: are not these magic words at the heart of the Christian conception of life? How is it then that we find them annexed by the non-Christian conscience of our time?

But in this same appeal we shall have recognized—its formulas are seductive but ambiguous—that kind of moral pantheism which leads to immoralism. It is to be feared that such blind trust in vital impulses, even when accompanied by a general caution against disorder and anarchy, opens the way to the most self-centred instincts and to those least constructive of the personality. Every man, following his subjective apprehension of life, will fashion his own morality. A Christian, of course, cannot look at things in this way. Nor can it—however alluring to youthful vitality—be justified even on the level of purely human judgement. And in any case, the second accusation convicts this vitalistic individualism of falsehood.

THE CHRISTIAN CODE DEFIES HISTORY

From a different standpoint, we are told that our morality has failed to integrate the new dimension of modern man, collective man involved in a history. Its precepts are anachronisms, unadapted to the complexities of the present world. If applied it may give an entirely individual illusion of salvation and a good conscience, but in fact a moral system of this kind has lost touch with reality.

Is this accusation valid? We are bound to admit that it does in fact brand one of the generalized deficiencies in Christian behaviour. And it will do good if it proves disturbing. For what a gap exists between the mammoth problems of collective mankind and the childish moral attitude of so many of us! Still, the assertion cannot be accepted that the choice between the personal field of moral dynamism and its collective field affords the sole alternative: the personal coherence of my life, however involved in collective co-ordinates, is not lost in them. I cannot just say: "Whatever I consider to be in the current of history and of assistance in human progress is good: the rest does not matter."

Accusations come, then, from every quarter, and in the name of systems which, in some respect, cannot be mutually reconciled. We should take these criticisms seriously and not rush to refute them. Men who are as sincere and thoughtful as some Christians, perhaps even more so, live these moral systems; they live from the human truth contained in them. It is up to us now to answer honestly: does our life as Christians do honour to the fullness of this human truth? When it overcomes their elements of deficiency and error, does it do so in such a way as to salvage that truth?

SELF-CRITICISM

I think it will be agreed that nothing which bears witness to authentic human values and to man's spiritual vitality can be alien to the Christian. And yet, looking at Christian morality as it has been for centuries, we may ask: where is its spirituality, where is its life? I have no desire to draw a facile caricature, and it is to be hoped that few will recognize themselves in this inventory of the moral conscience of a young Christian on the threshold of adult life. What, in fact, has his Christian sociological education most often given to him?

A morality of mere obedience to the commandments. God and the religious society have decreed that duty consists in obeying. There may be something arbitrary about the commandments, but no matter; they do not intrude upon the development of the personality; they do not monopolize life.

No doubt this attitude smacks of legalism and servile fear, rather than of faith and love, but it has to be accepted all the same.

Unquestionably, a genuine rectitude, an authentic integrity, and a certain amount of generosity, often coexist with an attitude of strict observance of the law. Nonetheless, the attitude remains Judaic. Is what is valid for the moral conscience in its infancy still sufficient when it becomes adult?

An ethic of respectability. Is there a word in greater contradiction to the whole Gospel than "respectability"? And yet for so many Christians it has become the criterion of their behaviour. As a result certain spiritual imperatives cannot be fully implemented—the truth about oneself, for example. Impossible to get beyond conformism. Pharisaism seems inevitable.

A rationalist, quasi-secularist morality. Jesus Christ and the living God may be dispensed with, provided a supreme Guardian of the moral order be retained. Is the follower of Jesus Christ to be thus reduced to a Stoic sage, a decent fellow, a disciple of Kant? Moreover, rational justifications are deceptive, and then the absolutism of divine or sociological law has to come to their assistance.

An irresponsible morality. Without the sense of the deep seriousness of every human decision, without the sense of the interrelation between all the actions of a man and his inner personal life, the external world and history, it lacks also the compulsion of an inner life which consciously directs every action or omission into that proper relation of interdependence.

One can imagine the outraged feelings of many of the baptized, especially the young, when their pseudo-morality is faced by the systems just mentioned. What will they do?

Perhaps seek to protect themselves and cling to their "principles"—a position of increasing discomfort in the modern world. Or they may yield to the attraction of non-Christian moral systems, and do this not necessarily or solely for the sake of an easy life. Or, lastly, they may realize that the time has come to go deeper than merely external Christian observance, and to acquire a living Christian personality. For, in truth, the conflict is not between Christian life and non-Christian moral systems, but between a Christian pseudo-morality, a sociological ethic of a given phase of Christian society and the non-Christian moral systems.

DIRECTIVES

Of what, then, will this authentic Christian life consist? It may not be too paradoxical to say that no moral system exists in Christianity, but only a faith in the Christian mystery which transforms the whole life of the believer. It is no doubt true that a moral aspiration forms the normal way of approach to God, and in its turn Christian faith will confirm and fulfil that moral aspiration. But is it not shameful that the religion of Christ should have become so secularized during the last centuries as to be thought of as a mere ethic; the faith liquidated, the humanism kept and Christ regarded merely as Socrates brought to perfection—and when morality is equated with respectability to say even that much is to say a great deal. It is understandable that from a kind of revenge against this moralism, some young Christians, among the most serious of our contemporaries, should sometimes be tempted to relax unduly the connection between holiness and moral perfection. Since their parents had more than once opted for a Christian social morality without faith, their own temptation is to opt for faith in Christ without the morality it inspires.

By looking straightway with the eyes of faith at the God of Jesus Christ we shall know what Christian behaviour is, without reference to competing moral systems.

In the beginning there was the glory of God, that is, the infinite fullness of life, freedom, joy, love, eternal youth and light; and a fullness which creates and, when it communicates itself, transforms. The glory of God rules all things, gives meaning to them, and envelops them. In the end there will be the Kingdom of God's glory: creation and history having found their fulfilment in being drawn to glory. But at present and until then there is the work of God's glory in the building up of the Christian organism to which we are called to collaborate in the steps of Jesus Christ; and this precisely is Christian behaviour. It involves living the whole of one's life within the power of attraction of God's glory. And this is done by entering into the dynamism of Christian grace whose starting-point is Easter and Pentecost.

Thus, Christian behaviour opens out into actual communion with eternal vitality. Knowing this, can anyone assert that it is against life, or that it is alien to the reality of the historical process? Everything human is here, and something more than human. Moral perfection remains the work of man. But the Christian calling makes us collaborators of God. Have we entirely forgotten this?

UNWEARYING LIFE OF FAITH

Christians must also reach an understanding about that universe of faith which they affirm. Occasionally one overhears unbelievers being told, somewhat smugly, that Catholics are indeed fortunate; faith so simplifies existence for them. But, is it in fact true that faith supplies us with an immediate answer to everything, that the solutions are at hand ready-made before the human problems arise, and hence that an anxious search to settle them is an unreal activity?

I can appreciate the unbelievers' irritation when they meet Christians who, in the name of their faith and as members of the Church, seem to be owners of all the correct formulas for the settlement of doubts and difficulties and who are convinced that in every sphere of thought or action the solutions have been found and catalogued.

But is this really the life of faith? One might observe, to begin with, that in their undisturbed repose these believers are to some extent victims of verbalism: they have ready-made solutions for every problem only by a studied evasion, a virtual denial of the existence of problems at all. For honest reflection on existence as a believer ought to convince us that although there is room for certainty and rest in the heart of faith, it is never walled in, never rigidly established, never labelled, but always open and inquiring, always in process of renewal.

The incomparable value of faith lies in the fact that it brings me into communion of mind with God and the universe of his Word in Jesus Christ; a source of light and rest indeed. But it is a rest having nothing in common with the somnolence that arises from possession. The law of the communion between the mind and the world of faith is one of increasing assimilation; reality is brought into the inner life with increasing fullness. Can we call that faith alive which fails to generate serious theological thought, and does not seek to know more personally the God whom it has met? Will it be more than a mere system of orthodox truths? The mind of the simplest as of the most accomplished of believers is made fruitful, even jerked out of idleness, in this way by the Word of God.

Furthermore, every activity of the mind profits from the faith which dwells within it. Far from imposing its judgements over all the spheres of knowledge, Christian faith gives a meaning, a general direction to all human experience; a vision of the world and of destiny. It respects each realm of knowledge, each degree of scientific understanding. Belief in Jesus Christ does not endow me with intellectual omnipotence, but it does enable me to give a general meaning to all knowledge, and inasmuch as it stimulates gratitude it stimulates fresh interest. We have indeed to admit sadly that faith has often been made use of to justify obscurantism and clericalism. On the other hand, we should not forget the record of intellectual awakening, scientific and philosophical development, produced through the freedom and dynamism of minds matured by the life of faith. This is an experience we all can and ought to share.

In short, for whoever lives from it, faith broadens the mind, makes it alert to fresh problems, even shows up its patches of ignorance. It draws nourishment from the most critical questionings and fears none.

Historians of culture and civilization find no difficulty in agreeing that, wherever Christianity has entered into the consciousness of individuals and groups, it has brought new factors and a new and untiring awareness. It is true that there are believers with ready-made principles and recipes for all occasions; they are proof against any questioning of moral reality. For them, all inquiry, hesitation or doubt is an insult to the faith. But do such believers in fact represent a living faith? Does not the truth lie rather with St Paul when he tells the Christians of Ephesus (and through them ourselves), that their "lives must be the manifestation of God's will", that they "must grasp what the Lord's will is for us" (Ephes. 5. 10, 17).

For God rarely provides ready-made results or effects a vocation at one stroke. He sows the seeds, sends out an appeal, decisively indicates the direction. But every believer must prove the details of his life in order to discover what the luminous centre of faith inspires him to look for and decide upon.

Thus the grace of faith widens each one's field of inquiry and augments his need to be faithful. I can no longer bypass certain human problems; I must shake off my apathy, and shed the sort of life in which nothing happens. That precisely is the adventure of faith.

If faith is life, how can it fail to move us to become living beings? Not mummies artificially embalmed to give the appearance of life, but authentic persons, really alive in the truth. This is our urgent need.

CHAPTER III

IS A CHRISTIAN MORALITY POSSIBLE WITHOUT GOD?

When we hear accusations against the Christian way of life—false if brought against that life in its authentic form, correct if against that pseudo-morality whose existence amongst us we do well to admit—we are driven back to the sources of Christian conduct in an endeavour to ascertain what is specific and original in it. We have observed that although the Christian religion is not a system of morality it does necessarily entail a morality. To the absolute "I am" of God in Jesus Christ, there corresponds a "Thou art" and "Thou shalt", and it is this correspondence that we must now examine at a deeper level.

The citizen, the wise man, the saint: these are three representative types of moral existence. Each bears comparison with the others. The citizen aims only at a morality of order and obligation; the wise man penetrates deeper, to a morality of ideals and aspirations; but the saint is called to live by the Gospel and the Spirit. In spite of this, public opinion often mistakes civic moral values for Christianity and, considering the wise man, it asks what Christian faith can add to this saint of humanism, this "saint without God". Both the confusion and the question are revealing. We shall try therefore to obtain a clear idea of this matter, the better to appreciate that call to holiness which is the vocation of every person baptized into Christ and his only possible "morality".

THE MORAL CODE OF THE CITIZEN

This code is not meant to be limited merely to the sector of civic activities. It involves the total moral attitude implied by conduct which is reducible to relationships of purely social conformity. Its imperatives aim at establishing external order. For such a citizen, law is beyond discussion, even though it may be entirely the result of human convention. Not that he loves it, for there is no question of practising it with all his soul. His concern is only to be on the right side of it, having done his duty and avoided sanctions. Possibly, if he was not observed, and in the absence of social pressure, he would not conform; after all, it is only a penal law. It may well be that, to start with, these imperative laws had some more or less immediate spiritual purpose, but the citizen is not concerned to unearth that initial dynamism. He has not killed or thieved; he has kept off forbidden paths; he has been punctilious in observing the religious practices of his environment. Long ago all this became just a matter of habit, and life goes on in an orderly fashion with a calm conscience.

Such a morality—if it can be honoured with this name—is pitifully shallow. It is hard to discover what is left of freedom or of the love of the good. Even the idea of any destiny for man is made questionable; there is no room for progress or development. The concept of good and evil is superficial; the latter in fact amounts to no more than breaking the rules. As for God, if his name does happen to be mentioned it is only as a remote guarantor of this legalism which distorts human nature.

This ethic of the citizen is without inspiration; it involves no ethical thinking, no creative imagination, no personal commitment. It is an elementary and artificial pragmatism. The sense of duty, punctiliousness, discipline, these are not enough to make it command respect.

What then can be said of all those Christians whose morality, confined to the commandments, is scarcely more spiritual than this ethic of the parade-ground, so indifferent to human welfare? The answer must at least affirm that anyhow it is not Christian morality, not even for children, whatever pseudo-educators may assert to the contrary.

THE ETHIC OF THE GOOD MAN

With the good man we find a real man. The word has lost most of its vigour in contemporary usage, nevertheless it does indicate an authentic human personality. He accepts human life as a promise to be fulfilled, a dynamism with an obligatory direction in which fancy has no sway. There is, he holds, a necessary truth that directs moral behaviour, and it is this which creates the human personality.

Such men take human existence seriously. Their continuous search amid the flux of life for a full account of its factors leaves an impression of coherence and harmonious balance, of a living unity that is constantly being fashioned. It all starts from an indestructible vital principle within the personality. This principle is hard to define, but it expresses itself first in a compelling ideal constituted by such values as justice, beauty, freedom, self-giving, and these are made effective by laws which direct them and designate their sphere of action: the supremacy of the mind over the body and its instincts; the intercommunion of the self with others and with society; the truly human use of the physical world. As these values gain control over all the circumstances of life and are applied by the great laws to every sector of existence, so the good man comes into being. The principle develops and assimilates to the ideal everything which human freedom encounters. Everything that evades this coherence or that does not submit to the control of this life-enhancing dynamism, is wrong; wrong and not merely an infringement of the rules. The good man suffers from his own cowardice and egoism; wrong-doing is an unhappiness to him.

A man like this, who makes his existence a harmonious

and free creation of the spirit, may surely be called happy. The harmony is with his conscience, and also with God, the source of conscience, the centre of all spiritual creation.

It is a happy thing even to take such a moral goal as an ideal, in spite of the obstacles that hinder its achievement. For, admittedly, men of this kind are not plentiful and integral humanism resembles a promise that is never kept. A man's fidelity to his inner drive is a difficult affair; idleness and cowardice lie in wait. And even when he has overcome self-deception about his essential purpose, he has no guarantee against errors of conscience or illusions about his freedom.

CHRISTIAN HOLINESS

This then is a man, such as ought to be the natural development of the human creature. Can we now import the notion of "saint" and call such a man a "saint without God", a saint of humanism, retaining all that is good in Christian manhood, but free from religious bondage? It would not seem so, for although this is a man of the spirit, he is not a saint. A saint is something quite different, absolutely different, since in his case it is God who has become the principal Actor and not man conscientiously seeking perfection. The Living God comes on the scene, in Jesus Christ and in the Holy Spirit.

Was God then absent from the life of the good man? Is it even possible that he could have been totally absent? Manifestly not; there must be an absolute source corresponding to the moral ideal and to love. But although the good man may have obeyed it, he may not have realized it consciously. St Paul says:

> As for the Gentiles, though they have no law to guide them, there are times when they carry out the precepts of the law unbidden, finding in their own natures a rule to guide them, in default of any other rule; and this shows that the obligations of the law are written in their hearts; their

conscience utters its own testimony, and when they dispute with one another they find themselves condemning this, approving that. (Rom. 2. 14–16.)

The good man certainly cannot know the God whom we adore. "We adore that which we know" (John 4. 22). If, however, he is acutely aware of human weakness and is set on following his conscience, may we not say that it was to him that Christ spoke in the words: "He who does the truth comes to the light"?

Should the good man meet Christ as the Saviour of human frailty in what will he change his behaviour? How different will his conversion to Christ make him? It might be said that Christ will give new strength to his moral endeavour; Christ's precepts will give definition to his vague outline of the moral nature of man, and Christ will show him the eternal sanction for his search for human completion.

This is all true, but it is not enough. He will receive something more than new laws from Christ, especially if such laws are presented as decrees coming down from heaven. He will receive a new vital principle, transforming everything from its centre. We may recall Christ's conversation with Nicodemus: "A man cannot enter into the kingdom of God without being born again. What is born by natural birth is a thing of nature, what is born by spiritual birth is a thing of spirit. Do not be surprised, then, at my telling thee, You must be born anew" (John 3. 3–7). A new meaning is given to human destiny and a new inner power to correspond to it, a new and living purpose. Thus it is that the morality of the good man is transformed, as yeast transforms dough.

This living purpose is that of God himself, the dynamism of his glory and love, entering the believer's consciousness and so enabling him to dwell within the divine life itself. Man's moral conduct henceforth finds its origin in God; the living God has become the inner law of his life. It is to us Christians that the Apostle Peter's words are addressed: "It is a holy God who has called you, and you too must be holy in all the ordering of your lives; you must be holy, the Scripture says, because I am holy" (1 Peter 1. 15). And St Paul: "Be ye imitators of God as well as beloved sons" (Ephes. 5. 7). In thus telling us to imitate God the apostles are only repeating our Lord: "Be perfect, as your heavenly father is perfect" (Matt. 5. 48).

But God's living purpose finds its completion in love, it is the expression of love. Therefore, if God becomes the motivating power and the ideal of perfection in me, the sum of the saint's morality is love. As a result of his researches among Christian mystics Bergson found that it is love that distinguishes them from the good man:

> The mystic has felt truth flow in upon him from its source as force in action ... for the love that consumes him is not simply human love of God, it is God's own love for all men. Through God and with his help the mystic loves mankind with divine love. It is not that fraternity which the philosophers commended in the name of reason, arguing from the fact that all men share basically in the same rational essence. This is a noble ideal that commands respect, and if it does not prove too hard on the individual and the community, then one will try to achieve it. But it cannot evoke passion (*Les deux Sources*, p. 250).

However, even imitation of God and collaboration in God's eternal love do not exhaust the morality of the saint; the centrality of Christ has not been mentioned. For he who is absolutely and essentially the saint is Jesus Christ. Throughout his life he was the perfect imitator of God. He is the unique human model, in whom divine and human behaviour are conjoined; the unique collaborator in God's glory. To act as a saint, therefore, is to imitate him. Christian holiness is a mime of Christ, a continual imitation of him.

Even this must not be understood superficially. For the imitation of Christ does not mean the mere outward reproduction of his mode of life. Jesus Christ is alive; the power and spirit of his risen life is within us. We can say with St

Paul: "The law is Christ within me" (1 Cor. 9. 2). The source of the Christian vitality of our conscience is the spirit of Jesus Christ and, having this, the sum of our work is to act throughout life in union with Christ: I live and yet it is Jesus Christ who lives in me. Human existence in its entirety —life and death, joy and sorrow, success and failure, solitude and company, soul and body, all become tributaries of the mystery of Christ as it expands through time and space. The Christian virtues will diversify the dynamism of the imitation of Christ according to the various fields of activity; those that relate to God and men; to nature and society; to the various elements of personal life. They dispose the believer to the action of the grace of the Holy Spirit. Christian holiness makes us act within the Christosphere and builds it up within our personal lives. "While we live", says St Paul, "we live as the Lord's servants; when we die we die as the Lord's servants; in life and death we belong to the Lord" (Rom. 14. 7–8).

A PROVISIONAL CONCLUSION

From our encounter with the citizen, the good man and the saint, two results stand out:

The citizen knows what it is to break the rules, the good man understands the meaning of wrong, the saint knows sin. In the life of the Christian saint sin means every action that does not take place within the Christosphere, that evades the drive of divine love and the clasp of the mystery of Christ.

In the life of the saint there is no room for the Pharisee. His love of Christ and his brethren with his whole strength and spirit knows no end. Perfection is never attained.

All of us, whoever we may be, are called to advance constantly in putting this morality (better, this mysticism) of holiness in Jesus Christ into practice. We have no choice. For if the ideal of the good man is aristocratic, the calling of the saint is for all those who share the incomparable grandeur of being sons of God and members of Jesus Christ.

No one ever loves enough; and what believer would presume to assert that in this matter he was more than an apprentice?

CHAPTER IV

GRAVEN IMAGES AND THE TRUE GOD

In religious circles one often hears it said that in our time men have lost the sense of God. What is meant is not only that the sense of a transcendent Being has vanished from those without faith, but that also among Christians the sense of the grandeur of the living God has gone.

Words must be weighed. When we say "sense of God" we mean much more than the idea or notion of God. To have the sense of some existent reality, music for example, implies that it has been experienced, that there has been an encounter which involves the heart. Speaking very generally, to possess the sense of God is to have had the spiritual experience—something beyond words, ideas and feelings—of the reality, presence, power and grandeur of the divine Absolute. It amounts to this: a unique encounter has brought about a change in one's personal life.

There is no such thing as "religion in general", and hence there is no authentic Christian life without a definite experience of this kind.

If this loss of the sense of God among our contemporaries represents an accurate diagnosis, it is a serious matter indeed. But *is* it accurate? Or at least can it be stated as an unqualified generalization? Is it so certain that the generations which preceded us had a really authentic sense of God? And then, can this sense—either considered as present or deplored as absent—be taken as one and the same in non-Christian religions (the sense belonging to the "naturally religious" man) and in that which results from Christian faith? For although the same external phenomenon may appear in both Christians and non-Christians, that does not necessarily prove that they proceed from the same reality. If the pessimistic diagnosis is to be retained all these questions must be examined in detail. Is there a crisis of the sense of God among Christians?

What do we mean when we say that Christians today lack the sense of God? First, that they are victims of verbalism: God has become a mere word in the language, a name like any other. And the picture of this word in the imagination is a triangular figure, an old man with a white beard or even some over-sized ghostly vertebrate. The ideas about him consist of dim memories from the past; his was a name that was learnt too early, kept in mind and repeated without ever having come to life. Lucky are those for whom it does not inevitably recall the boredom of childhood's catechism. It is a verbal affirmation about something transcendent that is too remote and too vague to become really personal to the man who makes it.

Secondly, that they no longer fear God. God as the source of religious emotion, as supremely fascinating, seems to them something confined to primitive man. And they think that a God without any trace of a human characteristic is unworthy of the divinity itself. The avenging God of the Psalms looks too much like a man-made compensation for the fear that surrounds human life. It is a transcendence unacceptable to those whose religion is more adult than that expressed in "holy pictures".

In many Christians both these attitudes are found combined; in their religious consciousness God is brought down to the limits of mankind's dialogue with itself, and a particularly casual dialogue, intermittent, self-concerned, without subtlety and without wonder. It is a familiarity that is not the product of an inner spiritual life and lacks even that sacred quality observable in some simple but deeply human attitudes. And, in so far as God is still believed to exist, it is a short step to the mentality of magic. This remote and good-humoured Being will be made use of as a hypothetical remedy for human dissatisfaction or as a guarantee of the social order.

This crisis of the sense of God manifests the lack of spiritual authenticity in the religion of many Christians. It also underlines the muddle-headedness among Christians as to the very meaning of religion. Is it not true that fear of an alien and threatening God, and instinctive or childish aptitudes with regard to the holy, are sometimes considered to show a sense of God? Today, minds that have had a scientific and technical training are critical of such an outlook, and the spiritual nothingness which it cloaked is exposed. And hence one can hardly talk about the loss of the sense of God when it has only been a pseudo-sense. It makes it very necessary to know what exactly is the Christian sense of God which should be the source of life for the baptized. And to obtain this knowledge a preliminary critique of the ambiguous idea of transcendence is required and also some light on the incompleteness and even impurity that can affect the idea of the holy in its relation to Christian faith.

KNOWING THE TRUE GOD

If we would give back the sense of God to Christians, not just any expression of the holy and of divine transcendence will do. There are a number of authentic affirmations about the divine reality, and also a number of false ones. But even one that is authentically spiritual is not necessarily in conformity with that given by the Bible and Christianity. Many Christian deviations in morals and worship, much equivocal behaviour, almost certainly spring from the fact that the God of Jesus Christ was not encountered at the start. In other words, faith had not met its object. Under the cloak of the

Christian God the images of pre-Christian gods have got into the catechism and into Christian expressions. Our God has been given a false face, and to find what he truly is we must go back to the sources of revelation.

A critique of these masks of God would be valuable. The more so because every believer, however authentic his conversion, may quite well find that one part of his mind or himself, at certain times, responds to one or other of these non-Christian transcendent ideas as being more satisfying to the instinctive demands of life. From the biblical point of view there would seem to be both greatness and danger in the fact that man needs God. The danger is that God may be the mere answer to a need and reduced to the level of that need. Only a step further and he becomes nothing but the projection against the Absolute of man's search for security against fear, against psychological or sociological conflicts with himself, with nature or society; a projection also of his search for higher emotional states. Without his realizing it, idolatry and magic are at hand.

When we speak of a Christian knowledge of God, the knowledge meant is not that which is gained by having touched something with one's hands and measured it, in the way that a carpenter "knows" a piece of wood. Nor does it mean being supplied with proofs and demonstrations— "knowing" like a philosopher or a scholar. Nor, again, is it like that of a tourist who gets to "know" a town. To know God is to have entered into the world that is filled with his presence and to share in that experience by which he has introduced himself into history. It is to have recognized his face by entering into the meaning of the signs of his coming and to be united to his action and his person. At bottom, God is known because he has made himself known.

GOD'S INITIATIVE

Man has set out for the divine Absolute along many paths —poetical, philosophical, religious. This search for the

Absolute, this restlessness for the divine is doubtless the mark of man's unique significance.

Without in any way despising this, it must however be stated unequivocally that the Christian does not travel along any of these roads in order to meet his God. He is met only on the road laid down by himself, the road that leads from him to us. He has taken the initiative.

We often say: God has spoken; and indeed this phrase contains the whole mystery. At least so long as we do not reduce the Word of God to words about God or to the utterances of a lecturer on religion! To say that God has spoken means that he has personally come into human history and infused it with a new dynamism, that through many interventions and significant happenings he has shown what he intends his creation to become. How in fact does a person become known? Is it from what he says about himself, from his photograph, from his police dossier? There is a surer way. It is by allowing those around him to form a synthesis of his personality from the way he behaves, from the decisions he takes and how he spends his days. And this is what God did in the history of the people of God. In different but not contradictory forms he became involved in that history. The evidence that can be gathered about a human personality is often confused and incoherent. It is not so with God who is consistently faithful.

Finally, it is in Jesus Christ that God came unambiguously into history. In Christ he made himself known by assembling all the characteristics previously revealed into the unity of a human being. Every action of Jesus involves God and through him man recognizes the God who has made himself known. So that if we are looking for the signs that reveal God, if we seek his face, we have only to look at Jesus and listen to him, and in the unity of his person realize that God is near. Ultimately, we know nothing about God that does not come from and does not abide in Jesus Christ. We have not to discover him, but to recognize him.

How are we to recognize him? This also Jesus Christ will teach us—we shall discuss it later. By his self-revelation God has committed himself and in return man has to commit himself also. Jesus did not get to know God by the sort of knowledge that a traveller has, by information of a scientific, philosophical or dilettante kind, nor by any solely intellectual process, but by freely entering that divine universe where his own unique personality originated. There is no hope of recognizing God if we are not willing, as Jesus was, to be wholly committed by the encounter. And to the extent in which we are committed our knowledge will increase. It was on the cross and in the resurrection that the Jesus of history came to know God fully.

THE GOD OF JESUS CHRIST

The personal God and the maker of persons

Jesus was not the questioner of some vague deity, some god in the sky, "a kind of outsized ghostly vertebrate" in Nietzsche's ironic phrase, but of a God who was powerful and definite, totally and infinitely conscious, a personality of absolute perfection. The God of Jesus is a God who speaks and to whom one answers; a God who summons the human person in its entirety and, far from crushing it, creates it anew. In order to meet him it is not necessary to be an exceptional person, but it is necessary to be a person, and it is not unhelpful to be mature.

God who is a Father

A Father unlike any other, without paternalism or will to power. Jesus, Son by divine origin and the Father's first adopted Son knew and expressed this source of all fatherhood. He saw in him a Father intent on the exaltation of his Son, tenderly jealous, but without caprice, having no use for childishness, that caricature of childhood's spirit. He is, says Paul to the Ephesians: "the same God, the same Father of all of us, who is above all things, pervades all things, and lives in all of us" (Ephes. 4. 6).

How shall we come to know God as Father without trying to enter into that filial relationship lived by Jesus and without committing ourselves to that universal brotherhood which the universal Father establishes? For the merely verbal recitation of the first article of the Creed is not equivalent to knowing God.

The God of the Covenant and of love

Jesus reflected the face of God's mercy; of God who has compassion on the wretchedness of man, who has a special love for the poor and is not baulked by faithlessness and sin; whose love is exacting, but a source of filial, not servile fear. In Jesus, God concluded the final and eternal alliance with us, that is, he made his purpose to be merciful clear once for all; his love means that he is on man's side from the start.

His greatness lies in the fact that he is radically distinguished from man because *his* love is absolute. He is the God of absolute Love, the God of those willing to be loved with a more than human love, that is, the God of sinners and the poor. The extremity of his love is disconcerting; in Jesus Christ this love is seen given to the length of folly for those who had no claim to be esteemed. Throughout the history of salvation it is a revelation of his transcendence; his power is the power of a love that is incomparably tender and merciful. Would a philosopher have dared to speak of the divine mercy in the way the parables in the Gospels do? His transcendency is personal, it belongs to a generous, loving heart.

It follows that he who does not love cannot say he is of God. The believer is caught, inescapably involved in the stream of universal generosity that flows from God. No more closed frontiers, no more racialism, no more will to power. That is the logical outcome of faith in a God of love. St John states it thus: "No one can love without being born of

God, and knowing God. How can the man who has no love
have any knowledge of God, since God is love?" (1 John
4. 8).

The God of holiness

Jesus was on fire for the glory that comes from God. He
knew God, by communicating with the divine life, as the
Holy God, and that is why he could say: "Be ye perfect as
your heavenly Father is perfect."

In Jesus Christ God is revealed to us as the one who
awakens in man and who satisfies the beatitude of those who
hunger and thirst for justice (holiness). God's spontaneity
springs from love, his eternity is an eternity of life; nothing
can increase his perfection—and yet he summons man to
come into the universe of his holiness, into communion with
his own being.

Christ's holiness indicates both our own calling to holiness
and the fact that God alone can make us holy. God's holiness
summons us, whilst driving home the fact that we are not the
owners of the Holy God. Glory belongs to him alone; man
has glory only in him. The God of the prophets and of Christ
"fascinates" by holiness, not by fear and threats. What is
compelling in him is not the dictate of a tyrant; it is the compulsion that springs from the need to fulfil a superhuman
destiny. The fear he inspires in a believer is not the servant's
fear of an alien master, but that filial fear which is afraid of
not coming up to God's expectations, of failing to achieve the
kind of happiness on which God had counted.

The living and liberating God

So Jesus found him to be, in his Passover. God passed
into human life in order that human life might pass over
into imperishable life and be freed from its connection with
sinful mankind.

He is not God of the dead, but of the living; the one who
must be trusted utterly, even when we are torn from the earth
and die, for to the dead he gives life.

The God of human history and of the Kingdom

In Jesus God makes himself known as intervening in human history, starting it on the way to becoming the Kingdom. He came, and comes constantly into it so as to make his presence known and his action felt. This does not do away with history or condemn it; on the contrary, history then receives its direction and its salvation in Jesus Christ.

True believers cannot be escapists. They cannot speak in the name of God and at the same time despise a world in which he has deliberately become involved. The logic of faith demands a committal to the world for God's sake and in union with him.

God is carrying out a single purpose for the world and asks man to collaborate in it. Plans for personal and religious security and salvation have to be given up in favour of this general purpose whose "architect and workman is God" (Heb. 11. 10). The laws and the structure of this building must be studied so as to get the right lines for one's own life. Caprice, fantasy and the pursuit of individualistic success have to yield to the activity of God's mission in Jesus Christ. It is then that God will be truly known.

In this process of rediscovering the real nature of God certain factors emerge which should not be lost sight of.

"We know that the Son of God has come to us and has given us an understanding of the truth; in his Son Jesus Christ we are in the truth. He is the true God and life eternal" (1 John 5. 20). Hence, in the concrete, to be converted to God is to be converted to Jesus Christ. In him the entire revelation of himself which he had given in the Old Testament is completed and defined. At the same time, it would be fruitful to start with the God of Jesus Christ and see how much he resembles the God of the patriarchs and prophets of the Old Testament. It would show the silliness of some of the oppositions that have glibly been said to exist between God as presented under the Old Covenant and under the New.

If we give it proper attention, the Lord's Prayer puts us in the presence of the God whom Jesus knew. The Lord's Prayer, prayed with Christ, should be an invitation to rediscover, with the eyes of faith, the face of the true God.

A further result is that it is no less obvious that not all the baptized see the same God and that the unity of the Church, at this fundamental level of faith, is constantly threatened. How is it possible to remain within the unity of faith and bear witness to it, and at the same time turn to these masks of God which can be completely false? And yet this is in fact what happens. Individuals or groups of Christians legitimize anti-evangelical attitudes by referring to their God. Believers, even priests, have profound differences about attitudes or judgements that are essential to the Christian life. A scandal indeed for unbelievers who are thus presented with a contradiction about the very ground of faith.

A personal scrutiny will however show that no one is entirely free from fabricating masks for God; from childish fantasies, degradations due to a cheap religiosity, idolatry and magic. It will therefore be useful as a means of purifying our faith to confront the truth of God rediscovered in Jesus Christ with some of these masks that threaten our faith, so that, with Claudel, we may truly say:

> My God, be blessed! You have delivered me from idols and made me adore you alone, and not Isis and Osiris,
> Or Justice, or Progress, or Truth, or Divinity, or Mankind, or the Laws of Nature or Art or Beauty.
> I know that you are not the God of the dead but of the living.
> I shall not adore ghosts and puppets, neither Diana nor Duty, neither Liberty nor the bull Apis.
> . And the "geniuses", the "heroes", the great men and the supermen, all these misshapen ones sharing the same horror!
> It is not among the dead that I am free,
> I exist among the things which are . . .

A LESSON FROM CONTEMPORARY ATHEISM

It is a sad platitude to say that atheism is widespread in the modern world. Here we shall not go into details about it. Our concern with it is only in so far as it serves to awaken faith and cleanse it quite as much as it tempts to atheism. Paradoxical as it may sound, contemporary atheism carries a message and a meaning for believers inasmuch as it rejects those non-Christian features which disfigure God and which Christians have come to accept. In early days some Christians did not hesitate to call themselves atheists, meaning by that that they refused their adhesion to the gods of the time. Today Christians might say that they are atheists with the atheists precisely to the extent and to that extent alone in which atheism does not involve a refusal of the True God.

There are three main contemporary forms of atheism:

Atheism from indifference

This is due to the complexity of modern life added to the spiritual idleness of most men who are content to live superficially. It is difficult to separate what is morally sinful in this kind of atheism from what should be ascribed to the inhumanity of conditions of life so brutalizing as to inhibit any reflection beyond that which is concerned with the primary needs of existence. It is a form that has always existed, but it has considerably increased in modern times. A *de facto*, a practical atheism, which does not imply that any critical attitude has been taken up about God; it is like a secretion within an extraordinarily anthropocentric world, a civilization wherein man is still maladjusted, a secularized society. Believers must bear witness to something beyond this atheism by drawing attention to the fact that God has called them.

The atheism of the mature

Modern man, with some justification, feels himself to have reached maturity. And this makes him consider childhood's questions as relegated to the catalogue and the dimensions of a children's world as unacceptable. Since he thinks that God is a function of such a children's world, and that this God corresponds to the needs of men not yet grown up, he, too, is relegated to this category—at least the "sociologized" God of so-called Christians, a God confined to the catechism and the sacristy. For many of our so-called atheists are in reality looking for a God with less alloy. A tragic misunderstanding is involved.

The atheism of aggressive anti-theists

This is illustrated by Nietzsche, Marx, Sartre and others, even though their systems differ. Sometimes it only indicates passion and ideological militancy added to the atheism of "the mature". But it often means more: the search for a positive conversion of the Absolute as God into the Absolute as man within the historical process, together with hatred of this divine competitor, who is disqualified so that he can be eliminated.

These three forms of atheism have doubtless certain common roots and arise from circumstances peculiar to them. For us "the atheism of the mature" is the chief concern. Its refusals will throw light upon our own as well as upon our acceptance of the true God.

Briefly this form of atheism rejects a merely utilitarian God, one who is just an auxiliary motor for worldly security, who makes up for what is lacking in the undeveloped, the idle, the unlucky or the frustrated man. Modern atheism is inevitably a threat to the survival of such a God, for every advance in human maturity means that he becomes partially discredited. Of course the atheist may be wrong in supposing that, under these indefensible externals, there cannot be a genuine adhesion to a more genuine God. For Christians God is seldom so degraded as to be merely an added support to earthly security. On the other hand, is it so rare for God to be thought of by believers as chiefly that and primarily that?

We shall now examine those characteristics of God which atheism rejects; they are related to the various resting-places of human security, for the possession of which God is invoked—or invented.

The cosmological God

He it is who guarantees the human securities of children and primitives whose universe is primarily nature and its phenomena. His power is essentially that of a demiurge and is not moral. Rain and fine weather depend on him. In the child he arouses a sacred terror, as much or more psychological than metaphysical. The dependence of primitive man is total. As man becomes civilized and sees his dependence upon technical forces to be not mysterious and divine, but explicable, that totality shrinks. In primitive religion the religious sense is ambiguous. An attempt to trap God and to escape from his anger is made. Conversion to him is not thought of; is he indeed a person? Miracles as wonders, not as signs, are what is expected from him. The God of the Bible has nothing in common with this demiurge, for although he shows his power in the physical universe, he does so in order to manifest a sign to a people whose existence is circumscribed by that universe. Through their response to that sign he begins their history which is also an achievement of salvation.

The God of feeling

The biblical expression, "God of consolation", is invoked, somewhat unduly, to support this idea. He is the God of aesthetes, romantics, emotionalists, of all those who use God as a security for the powers of feeling or for their exaltation.

He answers to the need for beauty (which easily becomes pantheist) or for higher emotional states. He is made use of intermittently as a source of feeling or of consolation amid the hardships of life. A God of escapism and folklore. Real life is not his affair. He is the giver of feeling, but his clients do not make him the master of their lives. "The beauty of religion", as the phrase runs.

A careful distinction is necessary between religious feeling (often degenerating into sentimentality) easily acquired by persons of quick sensibility and by those who are naturally religious, and faith which, beyond all temperamental differences, is a free conversion of the whole personality to the person and mystery of Jesus Christ.

Alert youngsters easily acquire a religion of the God of beauty. Christian faith can make this mature and so ensure its balanced development.

It is in any case one thing for a believer to praise God and give thanks for the beauty of his creation and of his redeeming work—that is the content of St Francis's Canticle of Creation—and quite another, to take up the attitude of Giono, Rilke, Saint-Exupéry or Chateaubriand.

The God of reason

This is not the God of real philosophers who is of greater stature. It is the God who is used as a guarantee in the order of abstract ideas, of the social system's security, in case it fails. Once again, this God has nothing to do with life.

The God of ethical legality

This God is the guarantee of an ethic whose sanction is merely social, of use in endowing with authority those obligations we think it desirable that children should respect; a tutor to inculcate good habits. He is not the God of the Sermon on the Mount who calls for conversion and holiness.

The God of the social order

In this case he serves as an absolute guarantee of a human social order that is valued for its own sake. He is used as the supreme security for some human constitution whose stability it is desired to maintain. There is no concern with the will of God but with society as made by man and contributing to his welfare. This is the God of right-thinking social systems, of manners equated with morality; the God of the Establishment, surety for the great organized collective egoisms, which the Gospel tells us do not constitute order but disorder.

The God of this-worldly Messianism

Here again God is harnessed as an auxiliary motor with the sole purpose of ensuring the success of an historical conflict. God will save the revolution and add a nobler and more dynamic tune to its motives. It is true that the relation between the Gospel and revolutionary justice is less ambiguous than the attempt to base a given social order upon the God of the Gospel. But the approach to God is just as distorted. Neither he nor his Kingdom evoke either interest or conversion.

The atheist's criticism of these unauthentic presentations of God is well founded. The believer, in fact, would share it; for the God they present is not committed to man, nor is man committed to him by conversion.

TRANSCENDENCY AS SUCH: AN INSUFFICIENT ANSWER

Agreement over some of the things which atheism rejects does not, of course, imply more than a partial acceptance of its position as a whole. When it has been agreed to reject any kind of utilitarian God, then the atheist's refusal to listen to the true God, as revealed in Jesus Christ, needs to be not so much refuted as transcended.

Atheistic rejection of the utilitarian God and of the consequent degradation of the idea of God in the minds of some Christians, may lead to treating God as purely transcendent; a unilateral emphasis on his solitary grandeur and on man's duty to be subject to it.

Some positive reaction against a degraded sense of God

is timely. But the reaction should not be expressed by a falsely conceived exaltation of God which, as a matter of fact, has been responsible for the degradation, and which has no part in the real greatness of the God of Jesus Christ. Examples of such false ideas of exaltation are:

God, the Great Spirit

Great, but vague; pure, but desiccated. He is concerned with souls only. In prayer it is the soul only that tries to reach him. Religion, in the context of this notion, has no grip on reality; it is a kind of idealist escapism. Jesus said: "God is Spirit", but not the sort of spirit just described. It must be emphasized that that "spirit" has nothing to do with the Spirit which Jesus is talking about. To think that it has, is to make nonsense of the word "spirit" in the Bible.

The Jansenist God

The demands which this God makes betray his arbitrary will for power. His greatness increases in proportion as his creation founders and as man becomes crushed by the weight of sin. The sense of being finite and the sense of sin in face of such a God risk becoming indistinguishable from that false feeling of guilt held by psychiatrists to be at the bottom of many mental ills. At the very moment when this God whose greatness is equated with arbitrary caprice is about to dominate man, he takes on an extraordinary resemblance to man. The impulse is to escape from his transcendency rather than to communicate with it. His presence, denouncing the nothingness of sinful creatures, is annihilating. He will get a slave's homage, a slave who risks no trouble with an omnipotent Master. In the Bible we read of God's "jealousy", but this attribute in no way justifies the idea of God just described. The jealousy of pagan gods, intolerant of man's growth and development, could not be less like the God of Jesus Christ. *His* jealousy means that he will not be content with mediocrity and that he wants man to love more. His is the passion of a greater love, not the passion of a touchy and threatened transcendence.

The God of cold majesty

Louis XIV in heaven! He is the supreme majesty that created the world and men in order to receive their adoration. He is the God of abstract religion rather than of faith. Man is never more than a servant and a stranger in his sight. He is served seriously and as a matter of religious duty, but whether he has any plan for the world's salvation is not known, and the notion of collaborating with his activity in history does not arise. Relations with him are cold and distant, purely individual, causing no throb in the believer's life. The ethics based on him are those of the commandments, not the beatitudes. Sacramental practice amounts to securing validity by the exact observance of rubrics and correct ceremonies, rather than in partaking of the mystery of Christ's Passover.

It is useless to appeal to the Old Testament in support of this God who is more Creator than Father. For it is in the Old Testament that we read that "God spoke to Moses face to face, as a man talks with his friend" (Exod. 33.11).

The God in whom there is experience of tragic conflict

With this we are closer to the Christian doctrine of transcendence, regarded in a literary way by men whose temperament involves religious conflict. This is a God who divides men in two, making them a battle-ground between himself and Satan. The outcome is purely eschatological; the triumph is not reflected in this life. It is a conception of God to be found in some sections of the Lutheran tradition, in certain aspects of Existentialism, especially to some extent in Kierkegaard, and in some of the novels by Graham Greene and Bernanos, as a reaction against an excessively humanist conception of God. But it is not the God of Jesus Christ.

PREPARING FOR A CHRISTIAN IDEA OF GOD

The requirements for this idea have been stated. How can we return to it? The answer is, in itself, simple enough: by returning to *faith* and not merely to a generalized religious sense or even to the natural attitude of a just relation with the Creator. Man is naturally religious, but he is not naturally Christian. The religious sense is developed by contact with "the holy", and this, under a number of forms, offers a certain transcendence to man, security and salvation in view of his limitations, the setbacks he encounters, and the impermanence of what he experiences.

In relation to Christian transcendence this need for "the holy" has both a positive and a negative aspect. It is negative inasmuch as it makes the religious man content with a mythical transcendence. Negative also inasmuch as it makes him content with a natural fulfilment to his search.

When the God of Revelation intervenes and summons man, it is precisely this natural fulfilment that is questioned. It is not denied, but expanded and purified, made to burst its shell and hatch out into the wider world of God's own plan. God not only wants to help men to advance to the limit of their own ideals; he uses man's profound dissatisfaction with anything on the human level in order to put before him a new idea of happiness and of personal and collective destiny. Even if he should feel satisfied with what the fullest human happiness can offer him, God still has something to say to him, and faith will have retained all its meaning, without the ambiguities of the merely general religious sense.

That is why the early Christians called themselves believers. The pagans around them were mostly religious, but since the faith brought about quite new relations with God, Christians felt a distinctive word to be necessary. Faith embraces everything that is included in "religion" and at the same time purifies it and brings it into a higher sphere. It is incompatible with superstition or magic. It has nothing to fear from the disappearance of certain superficial or childish forms of "the holy" that are bound up with a particular culture, an historical set of circumstances, or various psychological conditions. It may be that a period in which the religious sense is growing dim will prove to be an opportunity for a faith that is more specifically Christian and for a more authentically Christian sense of God.

God has been presented under many forms. As the Father of our Lord Jesus Christ what distinguishes him is this:

He reveals his transcendence not in being separate from historical development but in being thoroughly involved in it. Not through what remains a hidden mystery, but through what he reveals of himself is this transcendence brought home to us. And it is brought home not as standing in opposition to what is human, but through communion with man. In Jesus Christ God did not evaporate in the historical process, nor were human freedom and purposive direction annihilated. God's greatness in its entirety is shown in that glory which its power enables man to share, and the greatness of man makes itself known in its union with the transcendency of the God of glory, a union of such a kind that it may be said that Jesus Christ brought into history the practice of God's utter holiness. It is foolish to put a theocentric position in opposition to one that is Christocentric. The authentic understanding of God is given by Jesus Christ, and given in him, for unlike theocentric spirituality, the theocentricism of revelation is revealed precisely as Christocentric.

That is why it is so difficult to describe the God of Jesus Christ. For either those categories are used that have originated in philosophy—they safeguard the objective transcendency of the divine essence, but they run the risk of obscuring the involvement in history of the Christian God—or else anthropomorphic terms are used, and these, apart from being abhorrent to philosophers, run the risk of involving God too deeply in history. The problem is how to transcend both common anthropomorphism and the abstract concept of eternity without contact with time.

This language difficulty has its counterpart in the difficulty about the reality of the sense of God. Faith brings the Christian into a relation of familiar friendship with God, and it is precisely within this relationship that he becomes fully aware of God's infinite transcendence. But it depends upon the quality of his faith whether or not this relationship degenerates from a sense of being called to friendship into that sort of familiarity with which one treats personal belongings. The communion with God into which Jesus Christ brings his disciples ought to be the source of the true sense of God, as indeed the saints show. Even true and sensitive human love involves an intimacy which grows parallel with respect and abhors cheapness. If a believer's relations with God become cheap then the meaning of God's love has been missed and he is dealing with a graven image, not the God of Jesus Christ.

Without a sense of the basic frailty of every human value in comparison with the revelation of holiness in Jesus Christ, or, granted such perception, the refusal to make a choice because of the demands that might follow—both of these defects indicate the lack of a real understanding of God. Such a perception cannot of course be acquired by human effort: it must be granted as a grace. All the same it must be welcomed, one must be ready for it. And the only way to ensure that this will be so is to begin to live a spiritual life and to have an undivided heart—indispensable preliminaries for the experience of the living God. The way in which theologians describe the gift of knowledge, as an activity of the Holy Spirit in the believer's soul, admirably expresses this insight into the holiness of God which throws human glory into the shade.

It is urgent that Christians should recover this authentic sense of God. The world awaits it from them as dry land awaits rain. A world without belief needs the witness to God from believers far more than missions and meetings, far more than discussions about God, or attempts to defend his cause and his rights. The modern mind has been so shaped by the technical mentality, and is so obsessed by material magnitude and the achievements of man, that it seems to have become incapable of appreciating any inner reality, and hence incapable of appreciating God. Only the witness of men who have met God, who have become inhabitants of the realm of his holiness, who each form a point in which communion with God can be *seen*, would be adequate for showing our contemporaries that the divine presence is real.

"God is dead," says the unbeliever. "That cannot be true," replies the saint, "I meet him every day, and each morning wake up in Paradise."

The conversion of the non-Christian world would make a steadier advance if Christian communities, if the whole Church, could be seen as the luminous point where communion between men and the glory of God occurs, and if among Christians today there was the same intransigence on the nature of their God as there was among the faithful of the early days who are reflected in the words of St Paul: "Whatever gods may be spoken of as existing in heaven or on earth (and there are many such gods, many such lords), for us there is only one God, the Father who is the origin of all things and the end of our being; being one Lord Jesus Christ, the creator of all things, who is our way to him" (1 Cor. 8. 5–7).

CHAPTER V

CONVERSION: THE WAY INTO THE CHRISTIAN LIFE

It only becomes possible for man to come to know the God of Jesus Christ through conversion or, more precisely, *in* conversion. We have seen that knowledge of him demands that we commit ourselves, in answer to that self-committal in Jesus Christ by which he has made himself known. Conversion cannot begin until God is recognized. But he only becomes really known when it is completed.

Christian conversion is not something simple and instantaneous, it is a movement, a process. It is this that we are about to analyse, using Christian experience as material and with some hope of converting ourselves.

CONVERSION AS A FACT

What takes place when a man is converted? In a sense each way to God, each conversion, is unique, as stories of conversion prove. And underlying this uniqueness there is a common likeness which enables the question to be answered.

This is the general outline. A man is intent on human glory (cf. John 12. 43), the development of a human life from its own resources. Perhaps he has achieved a measure of integrity and his happiness was not wholly egoistic. He was looking for something beyond an all too human life and he worked for it, hoping that human resources would prove sufficient. Then everything changed. And from then on he based his life on the glory promised and given by the Living God, according to the testimony of Jesus Christ. The axis of his existence had changed; human values, formerly considered to be absolute, are now envisaged simply as co-operating in the sphere of divine values. He engages his whole life and energy in the service of a goal beyond history, shown to him by Christ. He gives up worldly self-sufficiency and the limited plan for glory and instead puts a total and active trust in the plan for God's glory in Jesus Christ. He still lives his ordinary daily life but with an entirely altered perspective and direction.

How did he come to this? Not by some sudden and miraculous inner revelation, for although his decision may have been made at a given moment, it was the result of many antecedents, internal and external. In one way or another, this man has met God through signs and God has spoken to him—not any God, but the God of Jesus Christ, become now the God of Christian development in history, continuously known in the Church which is Christ's self-continuation and which witnesses to him. This encounter may have begun by reading the Bible, by an encounter with God's message for our time, showing that the history of the people of God is still in process and that man must become part of it. Or, it may have been due to the question raised by the words and life of a believer, raised, in fact, by Christ living in the believer. Or it may have resulted from the example of a Christian community which through the integrity of its life revealed the secret of the presence within it of the God who raised up Jesus. Perhaps also a preacher, heard by chance, may, through the direct proclamation of the Gospel, turn a man into a questioner of God.

From that day when God moved the man to ask a question, a long time may pass before the day of his conversion. Challenged by God, stirred to awareness of his holiness, moved to give up self-sufficiency so as to enter God's magnetic field, a man will think and argue and even wrestle with the Person who has called him. He feels divided between the gentle persuasion of grace and human reluctance to change. And yet some change has taken place already: he sees himself to be poor and empty, he realizes that the goal he had proposed for himself was brittle, that life contains whole spheres which hitherto had been shaded from him. He no longer trifles with God. It is all a preparation for the decisive change. The day comes when he says "yes" to God, God recognized in Christ. This is not due to fear or weakness but because God was stronger and more alive than he. God had converted him and he had become converted to God. Together with all believers he had come to the certain knowledge of the God of Jesus Christ, through that faith which would soon lead him to baptism.

CHRISTIAN CONVERSION ACCORDING TO THE NEW TESTAMENT

At the beginning of his Gospel, Mark notes (1. 14–15) that after John had been put in prison, Jesus came into Galilee proclaiming the Good News of God. "The appointed time has come," he said, "and the kingdom of God is at hand; repent and believe the Gospel."

This summons to conversion, bound up with the proclamation of the Kingdom and with faith in salvation through Christ, forms, in the minds of the New Testament, the clue to what Christianity is and provides the only entrance to it. Therefore the idea of the "conversion of the heart", in the Gospel sense, deserves to be studied as thoroughly as possible.

At the start there is a difficulty about the translation of the Greek word μετάνοια which the New Testament writers use. It is a word full of biblical overtones and these are lost in such translations as "repentance", "newness of mind", "penitence". Even the word "conversion" by itself, and without the qualification "conversion *of the heart*", can be equivocal. In fact when all translations have been tried, one wonders whether it would not be better to make "metanoia" an English word! Literally it signifies a change of mentality ($\nu o\hat{v}s$ = mind with $\mu\epsilon\tau\alpha$ = change) and it implies the passing over of a man called by God from a world without salvation to the world of salvation in Christ.

In the New Testament the word "metanoia" is used to indicate (1) the whole process, (2) one of its stages, (3) God's call to conversion, (4) man's answer, (5) man's first conversion, (6) his conversion as a return after falling into unbelief, or his initial conversion becoming more intense. Always, however, the complete process included three stages due to three gifts of God's grace: (1) the stage of enlightenment, (2) that of repentance or penitence, and (3) communion. Strictly, the word conversion may be confined to the last stage, but it must have included enlightenment and penitence. Conversion of heart may also be taken—as in this book—to cover the whole process of metanoia in its three dynamically related stages.

In the Bible "the heart" is considered to be the subject of conversion. It is necessary to have a clear idea of what this means before proceeding further.

What the heart means in the Gospel

The modern Western mentality has accustomed us to distinguish body, heart, soul, mind, memory, etc., in man. The heart is generally considered to be the seat of the affections, the passions and feeling. If we take this line, however, we part company with the Bible in general and the New Testament in particular, and join up with those religious philosophies of the nineteenth century which lead to inextricable difficulties about the nature of faith in the believer.

According to the Gospel the heart is the centre of the personality, the seat of personal activity, of mutual relationship and communion with God. It is in the heart that decisions are made, involving both mind and will, freedom and obliga-

tion, the moral conscience as God's command and judgement. In short, a man's worth to himself and to God is what
his heart is worth. With this in mind Christ puts the responsible heart of man confronting the Word of God for its loss
or gain at the centre of his religion: "Where your treasure
is, there your heart is too" (Matt. 6. 21).

Faced by the coming and the call of God the heart will
have to be frank. According to the New Testament it will
thus be either open, enlightened, resolved, ardent, obedient,
sincere, integral, expanded, wholly transparent, believing;
or blind, hardened, impenitent, without understanding, dark-
ened, uncertain, evil, faithless.

A conversion which is only a matter of ideas, an intellectual change, would not be what the Gospel means by conversion. An altered sensibility or a changed religious feeling
would also not suffice, nor a modification of self-regarding
conduct. It is with his inmost being, his adult personality, his
heart, that the believer must face the demands of the Word
of God. Then the heart that has welcomed the Word and
given it unrestricted right of entry becomes a heart in which
God, Christ and the Spirit dwell. "May Christ dwell in your
hearts through faith" is St Paul's hope for the Ephesians
(3. 17). Thus the entire process of metanoia-conversion takes
place fundamentally at the level of the heart. It is the heart
which actively welcomes the grace of enlightenment, which
rejects selfishness and is penitent, which accepts the Gospel
and knows God.

Conversion as enlightenment

This grace is given not merely to throw light on human
nature and its values, but more particularly to create an
awareness of impoverishment and sin seen in the light of
God's nature made known as a call to holiness. A man comes
to realize what demands life within the sphere of the divine
Covenant will make upon him, what kind of life God wants
him to live, and so, whatever his previous relations with God

may have been, he now sees the truth of his position. He was a sinner beforehand, but now he knows it. And this knowledge is a gift, a grace, for God who grants him this enlightenment, this true humility, does so in order to lead him to salvation.

Jesus, following St John the Baptist and the Old Testament prophets, preached repentance first to the Jews. These latter knew what demands the Old Covenant made. But they could not come into the New Covenant without dropping their self-satisfaction and admitting their poverty and sin. Speaking for Yahweh, Jeremias reminded the people of their infidelities with regard to the Covenant: "I have sent my prophets many times unwearyingly to tell you; return, everyone of you, from your perverse ways; do better; do not follow other gods to serve them" (Jeremias 35. 15). John the Baptist said to the crowds: "Yield the acceptable fruit of repentance; do not think to say, we have Abraham for our father" (Luke 3. 8). Jesus said to the Pharisees: "The men of Nineve will rise up with this generation at the day of judgement, and will leave it without excuse, for they did penance when Jonas preached to them, and behold a greater than Jonas is here" (Matt. 12. 41). And on the day of Pentecost, Peter said: "Repent, every one of you, in the name of Jesus Christ, to have your sins forgiven" (Acts 2. 38). To enter into the salvation of Jesus Christ presupposes a realization of one's sinful condition in respect to the God of the Covenant, and one's inability to get out of it, or even to be properly aware of it.

But what could repentance have meant for pagans who had never known God or benefited from the Covenant? God has his own ways of making himself known and of speaking to the heart of a man. Some consciousness of sin, some realization of the mediocrity of his schemes for happiness, comes to the pagan also, even if it is delayed until the moment when he hears the saving word. After St Paul had blamed the Greeks for their lack of attention to God, he adds: "God has shut his eyes to these passing follies of ours; now he calls upon all men, everywhere, to repent, because he has fixed a day when he will pronounce just judgement on the whole world. And the man whom he has appointed for that end he has accredited to all of us, by raising him up from the dead" (Acts 17. 31–2).

Even for Christians repentance must begin with a clarification of life by the criteria of Jesus Christ and the harmonies of that life which were perceived when conversion first took place. In the Apocalypse, the Church of Ephesus received this message: "There is one charge I make against thee; of losing the charity that was thine at first. Remember the height from which thou hast fallen, and repent, and go back to the old ways" (Apoc. 2. 4–5). The same spirit is found in the prodigal son: "Father, I have sinned against heaven and before thee; I am not worthy, now, to be called thy son" (Luke 15. 18).

Thus it is always in relation to the call of God and to the world of the Alliance, and through a realization of his own weakness that man is carried into the life-stream of Christian conversion. Awareness of sin will vary according to whether Christ has been known or not. For sin becomes evident inasmuch as it forms a contrast with Christ and the harmonious order of that new mode of life into which he leads believers. "No one can dwell in him and be a sinner. The sinner must be one who has failed to see him, failed to recognize him" (1 John 3. 6). But to have sincerely seen oneself a sinner in the light of Christ is to be already on the way to full conversion.

Conversion as repentance

Deeds now. Clarity about sin will mean nothing unless it leads to change. Penance must be done. Jesus, following John the Baptist, Peter following Jesus, preached repentance. "I have not come to call the just; I have come to call sinners to repentance" (Luke 5. 32).

It would be misleading to interpret this call to repentance as merely a call for better conduct and a return to the moral law. It is before God and on account of the Kingdom declared imminent that man is required to do the works of penance. The change is valueless if it does not issue from a change in heart. Repentance consists in shedding one's previous mode of life and making up for its mediocrity. It is vivified by zest for a different sort of life, a life that shall be God's; and no obstacle to it will be tolerated. Purification rather than modification is the keynote; purification so as to reach the end and purpose of conversion; the penitent heart turning from godlessness to the welcoming God.

Conversion as the "passing-over" to God

Enlightenment and repentance are the negative aspects of the heart's conversion. They result from the positive pull to a holy life and to the salvation which Christ brings. In itself repentance has no meaning. It has significance only as a starting point towards complete faith in the Gospel.

To be converted therefore means the acceptance, the total self-committal to all Christ's values and judgements, to his programme for happiness and to his demands. It is to be willing to have a new heart and mind—that of Christ. In short, it means making the act of faith.

For Christian faith is quite different from considering statements about God as hypothetically true. It certainly includes a definite acceptance of the fact that the true God is identified with Jesus Christ. But this acceptance must involve the active engagement of the believer's whole personality. Faith, as a grace from God and a decision taken by man, gives a different centre to the believer's life. Henceforth he is obedient to the call of God. Answering the proclamation of the Kingdom, faith has led him into the world of the divine Alliance that has permeated mankind through the work of Jesus Christ.

It is the Gospel ("Good News") which shifts man from his false security and calls him to repent. It is the Gospel which completes the work of repentance by opening out the new world of faith in Christ, the world of salvation. With this in mind we can see the meaning of the exclamation of the converts in Jerusalem after Paul had given his account of the baptism of Cornelius: "Why then, . . . it seems God has granted life-giving repentance of heart to the Gentiles too" (Acts 11. 18).

In whatever relationship with God one may be, Christian conversion always shows the characteristics of a renewal of heart, beginning with the enlightenment of a penitent sinner and ending in total personal adhesion to Jesus Christ seen through the signs he left as the presence and salvation of God for every man who opens his heart to the message of the Gospel. The New Testament simply gives definition to that conversion of heart which had been central in the teaching of the prophets.

When Paul was taking leave of the Ephesians he could rightly sum up his apostolic work in the words: "You your-selves can testify how . . . since the first day I set foot in Asia . . . I have proclaimed both to Jew and Greek repentance before God and faith in our Lord Jesus Christ" (Acts 20. 21; 16. 20; 17. 30). And when he was giving an account of his ministry to Agrippa, he said:

> First to those in Damascus, then in Jerusalem, . . . then to the heathen, I preached repentance, bidding them turn to God, and so act as befits men who are penitent . . . I still stand here to-day, bearing my witness to small and great alike, yet there is nothing in my message that goes beyond what the prophets spoke of, and Moses spoke of, as things to come: a suffering Christ, and one who shows light to his people and to the Gentiles (Acts 26. 20–24).

So it is that the Church of Christ until the end of time has for her mission the proclamation to all men of the message proclaimed by Paul and with which Jesus began his ministry: "The Kingdom is at hand: be converted and believe this Gospel."

To those already converted but whose faith lacks vigour and dynamism the Church has to preach conversion in order to arouse their hearts to a fuller and more constant decision.

To children and to the young who are baptized the Church must preach conversion so that, as their personality forms, a faith that grips their hearts will come to maturity.

To adults who are baptized but have little conviction and who have become merely conformist, the Church must preach conversion in order that they may leave religious childhood behind and practise a faith on a level with their age.

To unbelievers the Church must, as she did in the beginning, send forth a call to that conversion which leads to baptism, and send it with that urgent missionary appeal which the Gospel of salvation in Jesus Christ demands.

CONVERSION AND THE AGES OF MAN

The process of conversion that has been discussed is that which changes a man from an unbeliever into a warm adherent of the Christian faith. This might be called fundamental conversion, conversion in the pure state. It is what Christians mean when they call an adult who has received baptism, "a convert".

It would be wrong, however, to suppose that only adults who are baptized are converts in the Church. Every baptized child when it becomes adult must ratify the promises made at baptism by a conversion "of riper years".

It can happen also that a believer even after a serious conversion, may resolutely turn away from God. His only way back to God is by a second conversion.

On the other hand there may be no real withdrawal from God, but just carelessness in listening to his Word and mediocrity in performance. This may befall even an honest believer. Indeed as soon as we become conscious of our weakness we realize that it is the general condition of us all. It means that conversion needs to be continuous. There should be a constant "passing-over" from a life in which God is insufficiently known to a more intensely converted life in which he is better known.

Such are some of the different times when conversion takes place or should take place. The distinction between them is valid. And yet it should not be forgotten that conversion is a reality which must be present throughout the whole of Christian life. How much spiritual vitality can there be in that great number of baptized Christians who have never been seriously converted and who know nothing of God except his name! In the concrete, the great internal problem of the Church is concerned with the conversion of adults to a deeper spiritual life. This point requires amplification.

From baptism to conversion

In ordinary language we say a man is a "convert" if he has only received baptism when an adult, and that he is not a convert if he received it in childhood. The distinction becomes dangerous, however, if it is taken to mean that infant baptism does away with the need for later conversion. A true story will illustrate this error: a score of young people had come to be witnesses at the baptism of a twenty-five-year-old friend. In their eyes his conversion exemplified the completeness of the break, the gravity of the decision involved in the coming to baptism of a man who had hitherto been a pagan. The priest who was baptizing asked them: "Suppose you were not baptized, could you sincerely say that the certainty of your faith and your committal to Christ would be such as to make you freely take the compromising step which has led John to baptism?" Only two of them answered yes; the others honestly explained that their faith lacked the steadiness of a personal conversion. What was wrong with these young Christians was that they had not advanced through conversion to an adult faith which would have made them progress from the state of baptized children to that state of baptized maturity into which their converted friend was about to enter.

An adult who comes into the Church proceeds from conversion to baptism. A child must proceed from baptism to conversion. It is the faith of the Church which has stood surety for his baptism. What is meant, in this case, by "the faith of the Church"? Doubtless the faith of the whole Church based on the Word of God, but mediated by the faith of a particular Christian community (the parish), and even more concretely by those upon whom the child depends for its life (the family). The baptism of children presupposes the existence of an immediate environment of faith of this kind. And it must be added: an environment of converted faith, for a community of insipid faith will as a rule only bring forth conventional Christians.

The Church's responsibility for the education of baptized children should last until the time when they can personally ratify the public profession of a faith which involves conversion to Jesus Christ and the obligation to lead a holy life that follows from it. If twenty years or more are needed in order to form an adult on the psychological and social planes, why should less time be needed—apart from exceptional cases—for reaching the status of an adult Christian? Baptismal ratification, therefore, runs its course for some twenty years until the time when the child prematurely born in the Church reaches through mature conversion the position of an adult baptized convert.

Christian children and Christian youth need a maternal education which, following the rhythm of their human experience, awakens them to the world of Jesus Christ and to that of men, and which enables them to live in an environment that unites the two worlds in itself. At the start, the family forms this indispensable environment. Youth movements will, later, largely replace it; in them, among the older members, the adolescent will discover the convincing reason for an organic unity between his faith and the life he is entering upon. Social surroundings vitalized by faith must neutralize social influences that are pagan. In former times social pressure worked in favour of faith; today communal osmosis leads to unbelief. This does not mean that we should try to rebuild the social structures that belonged to Christendom, but that young Christians should be drafted into authentic and living Christian communities of their own calibre. In these their faith could develop in synchronism with their life and they would have that fraternal support which is indispensable in crises of spiritual growth.

The expression of faith in Christ always has a relation to the contemporary mentality and the contemporary idea of man. The education of young Christians in this faith with a view to adult conversion cannot take place in an atmosphere that is outside time or which merely bears witness to the past. Christian communities responsible for this education will be at the heart of present-day problems, for only then can they help the young to become steady and serious believers, witnesses to the indestructible message of Christ's Gospel in the world which provides the material for their conscience. When difficulties about faith crop up within the community of the Church they may well provoke an enrichment of faith, but met by the individual in isolation such difficulties could stifle faith.

Steps towards adult conversion

All education in the faith must therefore take as its goal that conversion without which there is no spiritual maturity. This cannot be reached in a day, and if conversion demands a personality unified by freedom, then a child is not capable of it. For an adolescent it becomes a possibility.

The reality of a child's faith derives from the faith of those among whom it lives. The child receives and accepts that faith. In the same way, its freedom consists in sharing in the acts of choice made by the adults to whom it is related.

The freedom that accompanies adolescence confronts the faith of childhood with its first discoveries; subjective discoveries of emotional power, of reflection and idealism, of the body and its passions. Will the adolescent allow himself to be submerged in the experimental inventory of this inner wealth? Will he have doubts about accepting Jesus Christ as Master of his life because that might involve the renunciation of these exciting discoveries? Or will he freely submit the new-found resources of his youth to Christ and thus undergo his first conversion?

As manhood approaches the adolescent's faith has something fresh to face, as a step to its further development. God now calls not with reference to his subjective forces but to the facts of adult life with which his freedom will have to cope— with work, love, creative activity in a developing world, the formation of a social personality. He still retains the emotions and idealism of adolescence—will he now risk a deeper conversion that will allow Christ to be the ultimate and absolute meaning of all his adult life now looming ahead? Will he choose to belong resolutely to Christ, rather than yield to the solicitations of the pagan life around him, whilst the dwarfish faith of his childhood and youth is kept retired in some nook of his personality? The time has come when Christ speaks unmistakably to his freedom of choice and his whole personality. His "heart" is summoned to declare itself and be converted.

Some Christians, baptized in childhood, manage to advance through these stages harmoniously and, without dangerous encounters and crises, reach a steady condition of adult conversion that runs parallel with their human maturity. But for many the conflict is more serious; they may have drifted from the faith for a time, and then it will be something in the business of life, a question of social conduct or of love that will recall them to the problem of God. Another may be living on an inherited faith, knowing his religion, but knowing little about God, and then the conversion of a friend may cause him to reflect, and the dry bones of his faith to put on flesh by a personal conversion. Yet another may be shaken out of his somnolence by a miracle he witnesses.

Enlightenment is disturbing, and it is by such disturbance that adults most often are moved to conversion. The process is in part analogous to that of the unbeliever as he approaches fundamental conversion. We should not count on the aptitudes of the instinctively religious temperament, nor on those which foster primitive, atavistic religious emotions. These are often ambiguous, have little that is spiritual about them and do not involve the personality as a whole. Their absence is not an indication that a man is impervious to real faith. A sense of the holy is indeed indispensable; but that sense needs definition; not any sense of the holy will do. Only that sense of the holy which involves a man seriously in the most personal direction of his life and in his relations with others can be said to be a preparation for the Gospel. "The man whose life is true comes to the light" (John 3. 21).

It is still less a question of stirring up in oneself the primitive terror of an avenging God or the instincts of fear in face of death. Adult conversion causes a spiritual disturbance which only secondarily affects the sensibility. This is how Christ achieved it, and he was no romantic false prophet.

The truth is that for the baptized and non-baptized alike, the approach to the Gospel is made by living life more deeply. This deepening produces certain attitudes which form the right disposition for candidates for Christian conversion: the acquisition of a minimum of experience of the interior life which comes from attention to, acceptance of and communion with the reality of human existence; a sense of the finite and frail character of human life, that cannot even guarantee to keep its own promises; the humility of a man who knows that he is poor; the integrity of the searcher for what is true and real; making conscience pre-eminent and keeping faithful to the highest moral aims. All this forms what may be called a pre-evangelical disposition, a kind of pre-conversion. It is not the perquisite of intellectuals, but of those who have stopped being superficial in their lives.

How could a man approach Christian conversion without first becoming serious about the life he was living?

THE BELIEVER'S DIFFICULTIES IN THE MODERN WORLD

Christian conversion has never been an easy business. It is nothing else than a victory of God and the believer over the idleness, mediocrity and hardness of heart to be found in every man. They are expressions of a sinful condition which out of the conflict between darkness and light, sluggishness and grace, produce a constant drama essentially conditioning the approach to faith.

They take on new forms, however, differing with individuals and periods, as refractions of given cultural situations and conceptions of the world. Because of this a diagnosis of difficulties about faith at different psychological ages and historical periods is permissible. Hence the value of observing what are the social and mental conditionings which affect most widely the spiritual decision of modern man when confronted by the call of God.

Before enumerating and analysing the difficulties there are three preliminary points to be noted with a view to neutralizing certain possible objections.

(a) Faith is a gift, a grace. If so much importance is attributed to the human conditions of the approach to faith does not this indicate a descent into naturalism?

That faith is indeed a grace cannot too vigorously be maintained. No one becomes a believer who has not received from without the call to recognize the Word of God who is Jesus Christ, and from within the power of genuine adherence to the God who has manifested himself and calls. At the same time we should be careful not to confuse grace and fatalism, a gift and passive reception, the activity of God and his exceptional miraculous interventions, his transcendence and a fixed abstract eternity. The grace of faith flows normally in the psycho-sociological and moral conditions of the time and it is mediated through openness or blindness of heart. These conditions therefore ought to be known, so that they may be opened up to the Word of God.

(b) Much emphasis is placed upon the difficulties to faith in our time. Is it true therefore to say that the modern world is a world particularly opaque to faith?

We do not wish either to write the apologia of a world whose spiritual condition is not always an occasion for pride, or to put on trial a world which for us must be providential. It cannot be denied that faith was easier in the Middle Ages and that today it involves a struggle. But it would be wrong to suppose that all medieval circumstances were favourable to an authentic faith, while all modern ones are unfavourable. Later on we shall try to discover what demands are created by the contemporary spiritual situation and what opportunities it offers for the life of faith.

(c) Should the believer go out of his way to make his faith difficult? Should he not rather avoid unsettling questions and by-pass difficulties rather than confront them?

Obviously there can be no question of a critical attitude to modern difficulties about faith in the spirit of an intellectual game or from a morbid liking to be unsettled. On the other hand a passive or indifferent attitude in face of these difficulties is equally to be discouraged. In these days of the mass mind, difficulties about faith that remain suppressed or vague often prove more threatening than they would if frankly faced. In fact, the latter might well be the means to a healthy and reinvigorated faith.

Having settled these points, we can now turn to the analysis of some of the situations and conceptions which cover the various difficulties besetting the conversion of modern man. It is a changing and complex affair and the analysis cannot be exhaustive. Certain landmarks only can be noted.

The complexity of modern life

Modern man lives in a world which is too big for him. A synthesis is a necessity for a unified life. But it is almost impossible to form a synthesis of the modern world.

That this is not merely an arbitrary statement may be seen from a number of phenomena, which cover the daily life of each and everyone:

The physical and psychical exploration of the individual gives man an indefinite awareness of himself.

Scientific and technical information becomes daily more extensive, and this compels specialization.

The ever increasing growth of exchange in economic affairs conditions the whole human way of living and has led to the development of an increasingly complex science of economics.

The multiplicity of means of expression and opinion forces issues to hurried conclusions and is always making new centres of collective pressure.

The speed-up of the rhythms of history and life, the assortment and violence of emotional excitement, produces emotional anarchy.

The elaboration of the means to enjoyment provides new motives for luxury and aestheticism.

News of evil in all its forms now comes from all over the world and this creates an impression of massive fatalism.

The motives for settling the major issues of life have become so numerous as to create confusion, and duties conflict with each other.

This complexity of contemporary life has a twofold result. It produces an acute sense of the greatness of man and his works and of the rich inter-relatedness of historical experience. It also produces a lack of spiritual unity, a temptation to be non-committed, to be immersed in present anxieties and future projects, to refrain from reflecting on the meaning of personal life. Practical atheism becomes an inevitable attitude in a world in which the holy loses its transcendence by being swamped in human affairs.

It is also easy to see how any approach to conversion, which demands decision, recollection and attention to life, is made difficult in these circumstances. The modern believer must turn from heedlessness of the divine world, must stand back from the rush of affairs and get a more serious grip on experience. He must be helped to see the relevance of God to his life and the duty of answering God's call. He urgently needs to see Revelation as an undivided whole, vividly concerned with his conversion. In a word, he needs the Good News.

Anthropocentric humanism

Modern man in an expanding universe has discovered himself to be an object of great interest. He has become an enthusiast for himself and his creative work. Many of the powers and attributes formerly presumed to belong to God and to a religious civilization now seem to have become his. In former times the Church monopolized culture, moral values, art, thought, social and even political organization. One could not be a man outside her maternal care. Humanism today is no longer unopposedly theo- and ecclesio-centric. Man is more interested in man and his problems rather than in God and his call.

Conversion, however, is essentially theocentric; it only comes about through God's self-revelation, and calling, which brings man into conscious communion with him, and not through the subjective intensity of any natural religious feeling. How is man to be given back the sense of God's primacy, and of the unquenchable vitality and contemporaneity of his Word in history? How can there be re-created a passionate concern for God and his purpose that will include in itself man's passionate concern for himself and his plans?

The first necessity is a presentation of the Christian universe that does not look pre-adult or infantile. For the former theo-centricism was in fact somewhat naïve; God appeared to be an auxiliary factor in worldly success, rather than the God of the Covenant of eternal life, a God who was supplementary to a Peter Pan man, rather than the Being who summons adults to a superhuman destiny. We must regain the sense of the splendour of God and of the Lord Christ, the splendour of his plan of salvation, man's splendour through his divine calling and the splendour of that universe in which God established him as a responsible agent in the Kingdom.

Secondly, faith should no longer be allowed to appear to be an escape from life and human history as though God compelled those whom he brings to communion with him to depart from this world. As we have seen, the God of biblical faith is not like this, for he takes every element of a believer's life and gives it a new meaning, gives it an eternal responsibility without withdrawing it from this life. Every aspect of Christian dogma has vital consequences for the believer, a deepening and a broadening of his destiny. It entails the refusal of any God whose transcendence is alien to man and history, and a correlative refusal of history and man without God. Nothing is both so human and so divine as the world of Christian faith.

The technological mentality

The modern world began under the ensign of science and the scientific mentality. It is developing under the ensign of technology and the technological mentality. One need not be a technician in order to be spiritually conditioned by this increasingly widespread mentality.

Among its salient features may be noted an atrophy of the faculties of spiritual awareness and of their operation in the interior life, together with an exclusive evaluation of material success. This means an enfeebled appreciation of the privileged world of the person. Most often this leads to a quasi-insensibility to the things of God, even though impulsive movements from the infrarational strata of our being may be made to a religion degraded into credulity and superstition.

Now the act of conversion, like the whole life of faith, is essentially mystical. The Covenant with God presupposes a minimum of interior life even though this finds no means of expression. It is not a question of religious conformity but of taking God's Word on trust and personally giving oneself to it and to communion with Christ. This makes it clear what difficulties faith must find, in beginning and in developing, when faced with such an outlook, whatever value it may have as a corrective to subjective, sentimental or aesthetic religiosity.

Spiritual effort must be given its proper place again. The practical influence of the world of love and holiness must be shown, and that life with God can be a concrete reality. Believers must leave activism and verbalism behind and let the unbelieving world see the visible results of the presence of the God of holiness. The message of the Gospel made contemporary by the holy lives of those who live by the Gospel —that is the antidote for a world whose excessive technicality too often shuts out faith.

Ideological saturation

Modern man is a traveller. He finds that everywhere men have lived and are living worthwhile human, moral and religious lives, inspired by the most varied ideas, metaphysical systems and creeds. Every day he is offered programmes for life by political parties, sects, denominations, ideological reformers: and he is tired of them.

The temptation to be sceptical, to despair of truth, and to religious liberalism is understandable. Are not all religions equally valid? Is there any religion that is absolutely true? Are the religions anything more than entirely relative stages in the evolution of the awareness of transcendence? Questions that very much concern any conversion that claims to be absolute and precise, definitely ascertainable in its sources and expression, infallibly certified in Christian tradition.

It is a situation which makes several demands relevant to modern difficulties about faith. There is required a continuous pondering over what constitutes the originality of Christian Revelation. It must be more than controversial apologetics with its accompanying apparatus. We need an authentically Christian "kerygma" that will show the transcendence of the Gospel with respect to all moral systems, philosophies and religions. What constitutes the essence of Christianity and how can it be expressed? A precise knowledge of the content of Revelation, envisaged as forming in its entirety the one Word of God. An insistence, in the daily life of the Church, on what is essential in the faith, rather than on its minutiae or on particular applications to conduct.

A right understanding of toleration, that excludes both doctrinal liberalism and sectarian intolerance—following the apostle Peter's advice: "If anyone asks you to give an account of the hope which you cherish, be ready at all times to answer for it, but courteously and with due reverence" (1 Peter 3. 15).

Sociological uprooting

In comparison with the men of the Middle Ages and the following centuries, modern man is rootless. Economic needs, the changes involved in professional life, travelling facilities, make him a nomad without geographical or even family ties (hence the modification of the idea of the homeland).

The spiritual repercussions of this state of things are considerable: instability, a superficial outlook, more concerned with scene-changing than with developing loyalties; absence of a stabilized background and of roots. But it also involves a liberation from a world of merely conventional behaviour and customs, fresh experience, and a demand for a more autonomous and adult life.

In contrast, faith originates and develops within a tradition, within a corporate environment which transmits the living Word of Jesus Christ. A man who becomes a believer does not only come into personal contact with Christ, but also, by that very fact, with the people of the Covenant, the Body of Christ, in its progress towards the Kingdom. Christian faith plunges us into supernatural sociability. It looks therefore as if modern man is at a disadvantage in his approach to faith and in his life of faith, when compared with his ancestors rooted in a world of Christian social stability.

In fact, the matter is not simple. It is true that rootlessness and isolation are unfavourable conditions for faith, and all the more unfavourable because they come after a period of institutional stability that was somewhat paternalist in its forms. People breathed in faith from their surroundings without having chosen it, and then were abruptly thrown into an entirely different world. For many, such brutal uprooting is mortal.

On the other hand, fairness demands that we should admit that a society which is socially Christian is not without its dangers, dangers of a childish faith in men who have remained minors under the tutelage of their temporal or spiritual princes, not having joined the Church by choice, but being born in it, and remaining in it by habit, if not, sometimes, by social pressure. Uprooting, fatal to many, may at least offer a chance for personal choice and for realizing that faith is above and beyond every motive for social conformity and, in short, that it demands a conversion.

It would seem therefore if the two requirements can be reconciled, that we need to keep both the advantage of a stabilizing background and that of sociological emancipation. The Christian community meets this problem perfectly; hence its capital importance for Christian living in the Church of our time, as it previously was for the early Church. Christendom was socially rooted; it has passed, but the community has retained its function as bearer of tradition, and it provides an environment for the believer that is both harmonizing and a stimulus to emulation. But whereas the rootedness of Christendom ran the risk of giving the believer an easy life by dispensing him from personal decisions or by enabling him to belong to Christian society in a merely formal or external way, the rootedness of the community exercises both an internal and external attraction and yet allows the believer to retain his freedom and his conscience. In the community which is an environment of faith, the Word of God is constantly presented without being imposed by force. It is an environment constantly drawing the baptized to conversion.

Thus the rootedness of the community could neutralize mass pressures which, in an age of collectivization, often take the place—for the worse and in the opposite direction—of the institutional pressures of a socially established Christendom. What is called total evangelization aims precisely at making every collective human reality an environment in which faith may originate and develop through communal osmosis.

It will be seen how difficult it is—as we recognized in the second preliminary remark—to make an over-all judgement of the modern world in its relations with faith. It provides some of the worst temptations. It inspires some of the noblest demands which are difficult to avoid. Péguy was not altogether wrong when he wrote:

> The modern world degrades. It degrades society, man and love. It degrades woman, the human race and children. It degrades the nation and the family. It even degrades, it has succeeded in degrading, what is perhaps the most difficult thing in the world to degrade: it degrades death (*De la situation faite au parti intellectual dans le monde moderne devant les accidents de la gloire*, Ed. N.R.F. (1927), III, pp. 230–1). [And even more sternly:] The modern world is a newspaper and not only a newspaper. For our wretched modern memories are wretched botched sheets of paper on which the day's news has been printed every day without changing the paper. And we have become nothing more than this ghastly stampede of letters (*Note Conjointe*, Ed. N.R.F. (1924), IX, p. 93). [But it

was the truth also when he wrote:] If we will take an honest look at what takes place within and around us we shall see that in the modern world, or rather in the Christian world as it passes through the modern period there are (must we say: still? must we say: already? we must say: always) a very great number of loyalties ... (which) end in making, constituting, raising up a great monument in the presence of God and to his glory (*Un nouveau théologien*, Ed. N.R.F. (1931), XIII, pp. 100–3).

What then are these loyalties to which modern man is thus invited? We have seen that the demands made upon the modern mind may prove to be means of making faith pure and personal, more worthily corresponding to what is meant by an adult faith and conversion.

CHAPTER VI

THE IMITATION OF CHRIST AND THE COMMANDMENTS

St Paul remarks that the Christian "bears Christ within him as a Law", a law that is wholly inward and spiritual. Nothing is more opposed to Christian conduct than that servility to external commands to which we found that bourgeois ethics were reduced. St Paul asserts this strongly: "you serve grace now, not the law" (Rom. 6. 14). "It is by letting the Spirit lead you that you free yourselves from the yoke of the law" (Gal. 5. 18).

As against this, we are reminded of the solemn statements made by Christ himself, at the start of his public ministry:

> Do not think that I have come to set aside the law and the prophets; I have not come to set them aside, but to bring them to perfection. Believe me, heaven and earth must disappear sooner than one jot, one flourish disappear from the law; it must all be accomplished. Whoever, then, sets aside one of these commandments, though it were the least, and teaches men to do the like, will be of least account in the kingdom of heaven; but the man who keeps them and teaches others to keep them will be accounted in the kingdom of heaven as the greatest (Matt. 5. 17–20).

Are the Lord and his Apostle and the Apostle and his Lord in opposition to each other? Which are we to choose—

the humble fidelity to the commandments enjoined by Christ or the freedom of the Spirit urged by the Apostle Paul? Of course any such opposition cannot be maintained. Still, the question demands an answer and the believing mind must think about it. How are we to effect, within Christian behaviour, a thorough reconciliation between the imitation of Christ that arises from spontaneous love, and the observance of external commandments, whether coming from God or the Church?

Most Christians have felt the need for this reconciliation in their own lives. They want it to be a true solution, not a compromise, one that will harmonize inner spontaneity with the objective safeguard of the commandments. It is a question that leads straight to the heart of Christian loyalty.

THE COMMANDMENT AND THE COMMANDMENTS

First we must see what was Christ's own view of the matter. What was the exact status which he assigned to the commandments? It should be noted at once that sometimes he talks about *his* commandment and sometimes about the commandments in general. His commandment is spirit and love: it finds expression as an imperative obligation spurring the believer progressively to the perfect imitation of God. "Master, which commandment in the law is the greatest?" Jesus said to him: "Thou shalt love the Lord thy God with thy whole heart and thy whole soul and thy whole mind. This is the greatest of the commandments and the first. The second, its like, is this: Thou shalt love thy neighbour as thyself. On these two commandments, all the law and the prophets depend" (Matt. 22. 34–41). Thus the commandments—the Law and the Prophets—would have no authority without that commandment to love which gives them life. By quoting Deuteronomy, Jesus made it clear that already under the Old Alliance the conduct of God's children was ordained to something loftier than the merely legal observance of the commandments. This aim was completely reached under the New. Nothing was taken away from the Old; on the contrary, whereas the Old had been only on the way to love, it was now, in its entirety, given a new life, by being subjected to the unquestioned sway of the law of love. The commandments burst through their legalistic covering as the fresh sap of the Christian commandment flowed into them.

> You have heard it said. . . . But I say unto you . . . you have heard that it was said: Thou shalt love thy neighbour and hate thy enemy. But I tell you: Love your enemies, do good to those who hate you, pray for those who persecute and insult you, that you may be true sons of your Father in heaven, . . . for if you love those who love you, what title have you to a reward? Will not the publicans do as much? And if you greet none but your brethren, what are you doing more than others? Will not the very heathen do as much? But you are to be perfect, as your heavenly Father is perfect (Matt. 5. 43–48).

On this view the detailed precepts of the Law only constitute an outward expression of the inner stimulus to imitate God applied to the various circumstances of human life. The Old and New Testaments made up two stages in the development of the moral conscience, each being in continuity with the other.

Is St Paul's view different from that of Jesus? When he discusses Christian conduct in his Epistles is not the Sermon on the Mount the source of what he says? And when necessary he reminds his readers of particular commandments that show the way to imitate Christ in every aspect of life.

But when he contrasts Christian conduct with the Law's demands he is not speaking about the same thing as Christ. Christ points out the continuities with the ideal Law, the Law as it should have been. Paul indicates where Christian conduct breaks with the Law inasmuch as it had become corrupted by Jewish legalism. He had personally experienced the crushing weight of commandments observed zealously,

but without love. It was an external observance which produced first Pharisaism and then that discouragement which
comes from a willingness to be obedient that fails from lack
of spiritual energy. And that was the bondage from which
Christ's Spirit had brought deliverance. "Now we are quit
of the claim which death had on us, so that we can do service
in a new manner, according to the spirit, not according to the
letter as of old" (Rom. 7. 6). Having explained this, St Paul
could go on to speak of law and commandments under the
reign of the Gospel; it has changed their meaning, and the
inner law of grace conforming the believer to Christ has
become the one thing necessary. Through faith in Christ the
moral order has become mystical, the very opposite of a
juridical order. Paul is in agreement with his Lord; his one
aim in combating the law had been to indicate that in the
Judaeo-Christian religion holiness is something altogether
different from legalistic ethics.

THE PART THE COMMANDMENTS PLAY

The Jews had lost the spirit of the Law and had thus distorted it. Does this mean that Christ's holy ones can dispense
with all external laws? Neither Christ nor St Paul thought so.
For that would imply that the Spirit of Christ had already
so transformed us that perfect love was now the sole regu-
lating factor of our lives, that every vital impulse in us was
in fact a movement of the Spirit. It would be somewhat pre-
sumptuous to consider ourselves at this apex of sanctity! It is
prudent therefore to try to define what place the commandments should hold in our life, not with any intention of
deflating that mystical dynamism which is, as we have seen,
the essence of Christian conduct, but in order to protect it
from possible illusions and as a support to its development.

To begin with, it is certain that except as fostering the
growth of the inner seed of holiness the commandments are
devoid of meaning. If that seed had developed all its latent

possibilities, as it will have done in beatitude, the commandments would be useless. The more a man becomes holy and
grown up in Christ the more secondary will special commandments become. This is the reason why they take up less
room in Christian life than they did under the Old Covenant
—just as they do in an adult compared with a child. St
Thomas Aquinas remarks that "the most fundamental thing
in the new law, that which gives it its strength, is the grace
of the Holy Spirit conferred by faith in Christ.... That is
why we say that the new life is principally an innate law in
the heart and only secondarily a written law" (I–II, qu. 106,
art. 1). The commandments notify the law and publish its
precepts; they do not create it. (This, of course, only refers to
Christians, quickened by grace, in whom Christ's spirit
dwells.)

At the same time we do need to be reminded of the principles of Christian behaviour by an authority outside ourselves. Knowing this, our Lord entrusted the task to his
Church. It is an educational need; we are weak and the
energy of the Christian law does not straightway attain such
force in us as to regulate every aspect of life infallibly. The
commandments express in the form of a principle an application of Christ's Spirit to some major element of human life.
In addition, whenever one's outlook as a Christian becomes
dim and narrowed, the commandments are at hand, like a
prompter in a play, to whisper what should be done in order
to imitate Christ. To their educational rôle is added that of
an understudy. Like lamps along a road they do not dispense
with the road or with the car; they simply guide one safely.
In a fog they even become indispensable for inefficient head-
lights. We have surely all experienced some such fog in our
conscience.

THE CHRISTIAN CODE

We have been considering the commandments as principles
expressed as imperatives applying Christian ethical dynamism

to the issues of life: our relations with God and our neighbour, the use of our passions and instincts and of material
realities. But together with such principles we often include
their detailed application to particular instances of human
conduct. This host of applications, a catalogue of precepts,
customs, counsels, some of them going back to the apostolic
age, are really the Christian solutions to the concrete moral
questions of life. Through Christian education they become
part of our inheritance, and in each generation the Church
adds a further partial synthesis. We may ask whether what
was said above about the commandments as principles applies
also to these special precepts.

It seems obvious at any rate that a Christian cannot despise
this experience handed down from the saints. We cannot
expect the spiritual dynamism of grace to create a new
synthesis every time we have to do with some problem of the
day, not even if it is supported by extrinsic ethical principles.
I may have the intention to fulfil the law of love, but will that
be enough to enable me to determine whether I may accept a
given contract or enjoy some doubtful sexual act? Not always,
as experience shows. We may perhaps mistrust traditional
Christian solutions from fear of the casuistry which stifles
moral initiative. But that mistrust may lead us to discard
scruples which are in fact authentically Christian. It is a
danger that sometimes besets the most genuine Christians
today.

This ought not however to hide from us the opposite and
far more serious danger, that of a prefabricated, conformist
conscience in matters of ordinary conduct. A comparison will
explain what is meant. Supposing I want to take a walk far
from main roads. There are two things I can do; either
follow an ordinary traffic route or else consult a map. If I do
the latter, I must first be able to read the map and then proceed along the path formed by generations of travellers as
they made their way through natural obstacles. Even so I
shall have to make new paths now and then. The interpre-

tation of this parable is easy. To be able to read the map is to know how to relate the imperatives of particular solutions to the initial Christian stimulus which inspired them, to see the particular within a coherent harmony, not despising the wisdom of experience nor forgetting the primacy of its spiritual origin in the imitation of Christ. The map-reading is only a first stage; it does not dispense with personal decision or with the energy needed to accomplish the journey. So it is when we consult the dictates of Christian tradition. How many Christians there are who, under the pretext of obedience, remain content with a prefabricated conscience put together for them by specialists in casuistry! They have a false idea of the commandments.

THE CONSEQUENCES

The imitation of Christ which constitutes Christian conduct cannot be reduced to pure and simple obedience to the commandments as if that provided a vital and sufficient motivation. On the other hand, indifference to the commandments would bring some loss of integrity into Christian conduct. From this elucidation certain consequences follow.

In the first place, Christian holiness is a perfection progressively acquired. Absolutely speaking, the Gospel is impractical; but at least progress towards its goal is always possible. If we examine each Beatitude we can see how much remains to be achieved. It is a road that goes on much further than the lamps of the commandments can indicate. Indeed, with regard to some particular point, I may have progressed beyond the commandment, while still respecting it and still straining onwards to the complete perfection of the Gospel. Christ only asks me not to make my weakness an excuse, but to advance loyally every day in faithful love. Given this attitude one cannot be seriously out of step with the commandments.

Secondly, Christian conduct makes us free; free from the

seduction of non-Christian behaviour and free with respect
to Christian tradition provided it is accepted with the conviction of faith and not from constraint; free from the attraction of evil as well as from the law—as St Paul says (Gal. 5.
13–26) free even amid temptation.

Lastly, the Church is the educator of the Christian conscience. This means that her concern will be to assure for
everyone the conditions necessary for integral Christian living
which progressively approximates to the spirit and letter of
the Gospel. How does she do this?

By making sure that, whenever the commandments are recalled, the corresponding spiritual impetus which inspired
them is aroused and that their external observance is not
considered as all that needs doing.

By not adding to the commandments for their own sakes.
That would allow Christians to believe that in them absolute
perfection dwells—a view not favourable to the growth of an
adult conscience. The Church should use every means to
keep the Christian community from falling back to the stage
of the Synagogue, loveless, static, without complete trust in
the initiative of the Spirit. "If you love me," Jesus said, "you
will keep my commandments" (John 14. 15). Today we
realize more fully the application of these words to each one
of us. They are echoed by St John when writing to the first
Christians: "Loving God means keeping his commandments.
And these commandments of his are not a burden to us.
Whatever takes its origin from God must needs triumph over
the world . . . that is to say, our faith" (1 John 5. 2–4).

A PASSAGE FROM ST PAUL

From the letter of St Paul to the Galatians (5. 13–26):

Yes, brethren, freedom claimed you when you were called.
Only, do not let this freedom give a foothold to corrupt
nature; you must be servants still, serving one another in a
spirit of charity. After all, the whole of the law is summed

up in one phrase, Thou shalt love thy neighbour as thyself: if you are always backbiting and worrying each other, it is to be feared you will wear each other out in the end. Let me say this; learn to live and move in the spirit; then there is no danger of your giving way to the impulses of corrupt nature. The impulses of nature and the impulses of the spirit are at war with one another; either is clean contrary to the other, and that is why you cannot do all that your will approves. It is by letting the spirit lead you that you free yourselves from the yoke of the law. It is easy to see what effects proceed from corrupt nature; they are such things as adultery, impurity, incontinence, luxury, idolatry, witchcraft, feuds, quarrels, jealousies, outbursts of anger, rivalries, dissensions, factions, spite, murder, drunkenness and debauchery. I warn you, as I have warned you before, that those who live in such a way will not inherit God's kingdom. Whereas the spirit yields a harvest of love, joy, peace, patience, kindness, generosity, forbearance, gentleness, faith, courtesy, temperateness, purity. No law can touch lives such as these; those who belong to Christ have crucified nature, with all its passions, all its impulses. Since we live by the spirit let the spirit be our rule of life.

This passage is packed with meaning. It can be summarized in five words which in fact make up the vocabulary of Christian holiness: Spirit; flesh; freedom; law; charity. Freedom cannot be separated from the Spirit and charity. The flesh (or corrupt nature) is opposed to it; so also, in different way, is the law. Now for the elucidation of this lexicon.

Spirit

St Paul is describing the Spirit of Christ who dwells in the Christian by faith. It is an organic principle which shows us how to imitate Christ and gives us the power to do it. The Spirit is the origin of Christian conduct and the absolute author of its holiness.

The flesh (*our corrupt nature*)

This is neither the body nor sexuality, but the entire man, body and soul, considered as seeking happiness in the immediate satisfaction of ambition, possession and selfish pride. It is the origin of all false or merely apparent freedom.

Freedom

Not the indulgence of passing fancy or mere animal whimsicality, but the spontaneous inclination to follow the directives of the Spirit. It is analogous to the freedom of God whose action is necessarily in harmony with that love which is himself. I am free only if I am in bondage to the Spirit who liberates me. The risen Christ is supremely free; the saint is free because he has "passed over" from the slavery of sin to the condition of the risen Lord.

Law

St Paul is speaking here of the law which exercises an extrinsic control and compels me to conform; the divine law which is observed not from love, but from obligation, from fear of punishment.

Charity

This is fraternal love proceeding from God. In it the whole content of the imitation of God can be found. The Gospel makes it a unique command. A Christian no longer belongs to himself; he is totally at the service of his neighbour.

These explanations may assist the understanding of the passage of St Paul. As a Christian advances in holiness, so he becomes increasingly free. He is free from possessing himself. He does not abdicate his personality but he commits it to the direction of the Spirit who brings him into Christ's way of life. Christ dwells in him, his whole life becomes life in Christ. And since he belongs to Christ and since Christ also dwells in all his brethren, he belongs to them also, with unfailing love. And it is this that makes him free. He becomes free from egoism, narrowness, the instability of the world and the flesh and from evil. He can indeed be tempted, but not overcome. He is free also from laws that are a burden and from doing good reluctantly. Faithfulness to Christ may at times prove costly, but the Spirit gives the energy of conviction and the guide to truth. St Paul promises the fruit of the Spirit to the man freed by the Spirit, and that fruit is an experimental contact with Christ—stable beyond all vagaries of feeling and yielding peace, joy, goodness, in a word, Christian happiness. If we seek the freedom and the joy which the saints have found we must allow ourselves to be led by the Spirit.

CHAPTER VII

PRAYER: ASSIMILATION TO GOD'S OWN LIFE

It is a fact that modern Christians give little time to prayer. In ordinary matters they are obsessed by quick results and hence are not much impressed by prayer. Still, some would like to pray if they knew how, and they ask to be taught. It is not a technique of prayer that is primarily needed. What needs to be known is the basic attitude implied by prayer, and its place as a major activity in a believer's life. Briefly it may be said that, together with the sacraments, prayer at its best is an assimilation by the believer of the holiness of God.

CONVICTIONS: THE PREREQUISITES TO PRAYER

There are certain convictions about God upon which prayer intimately depends. It is opportune to recall them.

We believe in the living God who communicates himself and in this self-communication creates life. He is a God whose breath is the Spirit of love and whose utterance is the Word. Perhaps the least erroneous way of considering him is as an infinite personality. His presence, like that of human beings, makes itself felt outside itself and is life-enhancing. But it acts in an infinite, universal way, penetrating into the depths of created being.

God is almighty and his omnipotence gives life to all things, not only to the realities of created nature that come under his ordinary providence, but also to that "second creation" which is a participation in the hidden secret of his life. There can be no understanding of prayer unless it is realized that it originates in God's holy power and continuously proceeds from him. It does not start from man or depend upon his unaided effort.

It follows from this that the whole universe only becomes what it was meant to be through submission to God's creative and quickening omnipotence. The moral world, in particular, only takes on the form of truth, when it freely accepts God's presence. Man only becomes alive when the will of God integrates his freedom.

God is almighty, but also utterly discreet. Creation wholly depends on him, but he does not titivate it by unnecessary miracles. Similarly, he does not intrude his holiness upon the spiritual world even though he desires it to enter into his life. Iron filings are necessarily drawn to a magnet and similarly spiritual destinies are polarized by God the friend of man. But God does not use force. A man who respects the conscience of another will be discreet enough not to intrude and yet at the first welcoming sign will no longer hesitate to show his love. In the same way God only acts with power when some human appeal compels him to break his reserve. That is why his power is seen differently in the saints' lives and ours.

THE ESSENCE OF PRAYER

This human appeal to God is precisely what prayer is. Man opens himself to the power of holiness. It is a sign made to omnipotence by a beggar. It is a sign that omnipotence is waiting for, it may be defined as the act by which man assimilates the divine personality and holiness. This definition needs to be elucidated.

When a man prays he enters into communion with God by faith. Faith has created an affinity with the God who has revealed himself in his Word, who came into the world and remains in contact with it. The believer knows that it is Christ's purpose to make him truly alive. He also knows that for this to happen he must first admit that he is not alive and cannot come to life by his own effort sustained by accumulated created energy alone. The initiative and the action belong supremely to God, for only God can give God. Man can only receive. But his passivity is of a special kind; it is a welcoming, an opening-out with a complete frankness, and it means being wholly committed to God. Man comes fully alive. Nothing could be less like sleep.

This act of communion is a possibility because God is faithful. It becomes an indwelling of the Almighty in the human being who has called to him; a genuine assimilation between the will of the living God and that of the created will which he loves. It is not simply a psychological indwelling as in ordinary human knowledge when outside things come "inside", in the mind; it is an ontological change, a participation in the divine holiness.

This result of prayer is not peculiar to the prayer of petition. It comes about in all forms of prayer, for in all of them man is a suppliant at the source of holiness, a beggar confronting God, the life-giving centre of attraction to the human will.

With regard to the prayer of petition it should be noted that it only becomes real prayer when the person praying gives up being his own centre and instead makes his centre God, and God's will, and not his own needs, the one thing that matters. Prayer can easily become anthropocentric. The Lord's Prayer teaches us to look with Christ towards God and to make our petitions in conformity with the coming of the Kingdom and the reign of the divine will.

The basic attitude of prayer reaches its climax in the believer who is about to receive Communion. God is truly there, present and life-giving; but there only in order to give himself. All the sacramental symbols show that he is offering himself in order that the energy which raised Jesus Christ from the dead may be transmitted into the believer's life. From the opposite point of view, every authentic prayer is an act of communion with God made through the mediation of the Lord Jesus; it is a "Passover prayer"; it reaches God through Christ "our Passover who is sacrificed". He was and is the one being whose entire life was in harmony with the Father's will, a life therefore that forms a perfect and continuous prayer. All human prayer is included in his and in it gains access to the Father.

The life of Jesus was a continuous offering of himself in communion with God and God transformed it all into the glory of his risen life. Similarly, when a believer prays God enters into his life now and transforms it. The divine will takes up its abode in his body and soul, in the experience that has become a part of him and in the moment of history which his personal calling envelops. "Almighty God, giver of life to all who wholeheartedly welcome you, I stand before you and through me also the world and all living things. Energize me and this world. Cleanse what is sordid, burn what is sinful, hallow and make immortal all that is genuine. Do this so that my life and all life may deserve to be called the will of God and that all things may exist for your sake and be filled with your glory."

The essence of prayer is its action in assimilating God's personality and holiness into human life.

PRAYER UNCEASING

If with St Paul we mean by prayer every action done in the light of faith we can talk of life-long prayer. The emphasis must be on the light of faith. It is a misnomer to call a hum-drum life a prayer merely because it observes professional obligations or because some vague general intention has committed it to God. The light of faith must be as vivid as possible and if God's presence is to become a reality for every moment then definite times must be put aside for its intense realization. To dispute this necessity would be mere verbal juggling on the part of such a distracted being as twentieth-century man. There can be no authentic prayer without previous recollection. Jesus himself gave us an example of this when at certain times he withdrew into solitude in order to pray more intensely.

No doubt the word recollection, from its association with boredom, emptiness and unreality, is disturbing. Certain manuals of devotion and certain techniques of prayer have helped to produce this attitude, because they have made recollection an exercise involving mental strain, an artificial effort to obtain an empty mind: eyes shut, the head buried in the hands, the world shut out. In reality it involves a break not with life itself but with the superficial happenings of daily routine. For it is precisely life, the whole of life, which prayer seeks to bring into the sphere of God's power. And if life has first been discarded in order to enter a rarefied atmosphere, it is difficult to see how it can be made a prayer. Prayer among Christians today is in any case too cerebral—or too emotional in moments of "fervour". They ought to pray with faith, and that means giving a new meaning to their whole life. This faith dwells in the heart, the centre of human freedom, responsibility and purpose.

To be recollected means to be withdrawn from all the beings and things that fill my life, from the personal or collective happenings which make my present position what it is. Instead of being passively caught up in this whirlpool and almost losing my own personality in it, I pause. I take my life in hand and look at it in the light. Who am I? What is the real purpose of all these beings that are related to me and of all the things inseparable from my life? Recollection is indeed remote from both the senseless rush of things and from the vacancy of sleep. R. Guardini says of it: "It is not an isolated activity parallel with others. It is the only interior state that is good, for it enables a man to be in a true relationship with other men and things." It is an activity, not an escape, and as such is indispensable to any prayer which is more than the recitation of words or fanciful indulgence.

Some concluding remarks:

1. This essence of prayer implicitly contains every kind of prayer: adoration, petition, thanksgiving. One or other of these elements may in practice be emphasized in turn. But provided the fundamental attitude of prayer is maintained there should be the greatest freedom with respect to its forms.

2. Truly Christian prayer is not just any kind of raising of the soul to God. It is a "Passover" prayer that draws the believer's life into the dynamism of Christ's Passover. It avoids two pitfalls of which devotion is often accused; it is not a mystical escape from life; nor is it a mercenary request concerned only with what God gives and not with the holiness he requires.

Christian action finds its initiative and its meaning in faith. It must keep on getting back to that centre by prayer. A believer will see that this is obvious and will smile at sarcasms about his "mysticism". He knows from experience that prayer is the opposite of escapism, and that it is organically related to his militant activity.

3. Initiation into genuine prayer is a special opportunity for reminding ourselves that our sanctification is the work of God, of much greater worth than our own efforts too often made without faith. It is an opportunity also for ridding ourselves of moral subjectivity, self-centred ideas and emotional instability in the sphere of religion. We ourselves may change, but God is real, powerful and faithful; his truth is constant.

4. Life-giving communion with God in prayer presupposes a continuity, like all human growth, for God respects the rhythms of our life. We are impatient to see the result of our efforts. But it is only after a long time that we experience the radical transformation worked by prayer; the sense of

God in the depths of one's being, of truth flooding life, of the radiation from God's indwelling.

5. Lack of time is an objection made in bad faith. Not long exercise but qualitative intensity is what is needed. In daily life frequent short prayers are preferable to widely spaced long ones—if the whole context of life is to be influenced. Prayer has a natural power to relax tension and a very busy life may become deeply unified by its fundamental attitude. Of course its qualitative intensity presupposes an ability to become recollected quickly and a man can acquire this ability only through lengthy periods of attentive prayer. What the moments of daily prayer effect in transforming the whole content of life into prayer, these periodical halts for deeper prayer effect in making those moments real. The radical defect in this matter is spiritual inertia, inattention, and the remedy for it is faith which in turn itself develops through prayer. The faith of a man who does not pray soon becomes abstract and conventional; awareness of God's holiness vanishes.

CHAPTER VIII

RENUNCIATION: WHAT A CHRISTIAN MUST DO WITHOUT

Even a mere external acquaintance with Christianity makes it clear that central to its outlook and practice is that which is expressed by such words as self-denial, renunciation, detachment, mortification, etc. Today, among Christians, especially among the young, an uncertainty about renunciation is observable. In some cases its validity is denied, and there is talk of a "crisis" in Christian asceticism.

We must try and find out the reasons for this crisis in order to form a deeper judgement than can be gained from merely pessimistic impressions. In general, there seem to be two main causes; first, the forms of asceticism of previous ages are ill adapted to modern ideas and circumstances; secondly, the reasons usually given as motives for the practice of asceticism are vague and undefined. This second cause is the more fundamental and the first depends upon it. For asceticism cannot be adapted to contemporary circumstances unless the reasons why it should be practised at all are made clear. So long as it appears to be an external imposition, an artificial extra, unconnected with the inner drive of a dedicated life, it will be repugnant. For what and for whom is one to sacrifice oneself? Is there any real need to do so when life seems to be able to get on quite well without it? Vague appeals to generosity, duties invoked by what seems gloomy caprice will not convince and move to action a Christian living in a somewhat materialistic society.

We looked at repentance in the context of "metanoia". Mortification and renunciation can now be seen in the context of repentance. This will provide us with an analysis of the Christian reasons for renunciation; a brief analysis under three headings; faith as a solemn choice; the way of life involved by baptism; the fully militant Christian life.

FAITH AS A SOLEMN CHOICE: IT DEMANDS RENUNCIATION

Renunciation accompanies every stage of this choice.

To become a believer the world of whim and fancy has to be given up in favour of a serious concern with life and freedom. This presupposes the preliminary choice of a way of life and happiness, the getting rid of futile interests, the pursuit of silence and recollection. Some asceticism is indispensable if we are to rise above a mere dilettante existence content with the flow of feelings coming from every imaginable source, finding the absolute in moments filled only with fleeting aspects of beauty or pleasure, or in "success", or vanity. It is the kind of life depicted by Jesus in the parable of the Sower: "The grain that fell among the briars, stands for those who hear [the Word which summons them to believe], and then, going on their way, are stifled by the cares, the riches and the pleasures of life and never reach maturity." (Luke 8. 14.)

To become a believer in our time one must have the strength to forgo the solicitations of a superficial way of life, brimming with materialistic concerns, worldly plans, comfort, a plenitude of gadgets, exciting discoveries and non-stop emotions. This has to be done simply in order to regain the power to act with freedom and to make essential decisions which would otherwise be lost in the sands. The young, especially, must learn to estimate the experiences offered them according to a sound scale of values. They must learn not to confuse every novelty and fresh impression with the solid substance of life. They must discover how to secure zones of silence in which they can stand back from the passing rush of life. Such an effort is not compatible with sensual indolence and day-dreaming; it involves a refusal of many of the modern facilities for comfort, and it cannot proceed if the will remains enfeebled through the lack of order among the activities of life.

The point is not self-mastery in order to reach some human ideal. Life has to be given an entirely new centre, freedom has to be clearly directed towards an honest and courageous answer to the summons of Christ. Once faith has been chosen, our Lord's words will be found to be verified: "The Kingdom of heaven has opened to force; and the forceful are even now making it their prize" (Matt. 11. 12).

The detachment we envisage is rather the establishment of a scale of values than abstention from experience, for this latter, because it is unrelated to anything, tends to become a mere abstraction, a matter of words only and so, in the long run, tends to produce a feeling of resentment and doubt.

THE WAY OF LIFE INAUGURATED BY BAPTISM

The way of life that follows baptism is simply a process of continuous conversion to Christ. It is the progressive application of the meaning of baptism to every sphere of life. The Christian is baptized into Christ's death and resurrection. This gives him his direction, as St Paul points out: "You know well enough that we who were taken up into Christ by baptism have been taken up, all of us, into his death. In our baptism, we have been buried with him, died like him, that so, just as Christ was raised up by his Father's power from the dead, we too might live and move in a new kind of existence" (Rom. 6. 3–5).

As we grow up this life makes three principal demands on us:

It is a dedicated life. There is a logical continuity between conversion to Christ, advance towards the Kingdom and rejection of the world, and obedience to the Holy Spirit. The Fathers singled out the sin of "dipsychia"; we may translate it as that of a "divided mind", as being specially hostile to baptism.

It is a sacrificial life. This means a life continuously offered back to God, of obedience to his will, of sacrifice made for love of him and our brethren, in imitation of Christ in his Passover. This in no way fits in with the modern idea of "success". "None of us lives as his own master, and none of us dies as his own master. While we live, we live as the Lord's servants, when we die, we die as the Lord's servants; in life and in death we belong to the Lord. That was why Christ died and lived again; he would be Lord both of the dead and the living" (Rom. 14. 7–9).

It is a unified life. Every man's life and the whole of it must progressively enter the orbit of Christ's sacrificial activity. Nothing, except sin, is left outside. Christ becomes the reason why one lives and he makes our deeds a contribution to the coming of the Kingdom. "In eating, in drinking, in all that you do, do everything as for God's glory" (1 Cor. 10. 31).

Obviously such a life demands effort and renunciation, if we are to collaborate with grace. It is a trifle schematic—and no parallel with the previous trilogy is intended—but it may be said that there is a threefold asceticism for those who take their baptism seriously.

Firstly, a basic asceticism composed of reflection and prayer, in order to discover God's will. It implies a voluntary refusal of all superficial and capricious living. It implies detachment so that values that compete with faith can be given up—those "little absolutes" that try to gain a place beside the sole Absolute as alternative attractions. It is the continuation of the asceticism involved in the choice of faith, with the added difficulty of perseverance.

Secondly, an asceticism of expiation, an attempt to right the balance weighed down by sin. For sin always indicates dividedness, contradictory intentions, an effort to serve two masters at the same time. Where sin has broken baptismal integrity, this asceticism tries to reaffirm, by a decisive break with it, that the believer belongs to Christ alone.

Lastly, asceticism of purification that tests the purity of Christian motives and qualitatively intensifies faith's power of action over life. It is about asceticism of this kind that Christ is speaking when he compares it with the pruning and trimming of a vine so that it may yield more fruit (John 15. 2). Trials alone can enable the believer to know whether he really is living and acting solely for Christ, or at least is making progress towards living in unity with him. "A grain of wheat must fall into the ground and die, or else it remains nothing more than a grain of wheat, but if it dies it yields rich fruit" (John 12. 24).

All this can be summarized by saying that the way of life inaugurated at baptism, a life of sacrifice in union with Christ, is a life of such loftiness that lower forms must be renounced, and that therefore sacrifice is necessary in order to win the life that God gives and which he wants to mature.

CHRISTIAN MILITANCY: DEATH TO SELF

By this title we mean Christian action in neighbourly charity and considered as a witness to Christ. Additional reasons for asceticism now come to light.

If a man agrees that nothing belonging to him comes under his control except inasmuch as it is at the service of others, he can be sure that his inclinations and his needs, even his most legitimate needs, will often be frustrated. It will leave him little health and much anxiety. Detachment and the struggle with himself will mean self-giving and the service of his brethren for the sake of Christ.

This becomes even truer if he should enter into the mystery

of the apostolate. A martyr is a man who bears witness even at the cost of his life. Each of Christ's witnesses knows this instinctively, even though he may not be called upon to die. Christ prophesied that his witnesses would be a sign provoking contradiction, and would be persecuted. For the disciple is not above his master (Matt. 5. 11: John 15. 18–26).

Apart from martyrdom, the apostle—more than any servant of a human ideal—will have to give up his personal interests, his time, his status and his rest, for the urgent work of the Kingdom. We should reread Paul's passionate words to the Corinthians: "I have met with toil and weariness, so often been sleepless, hungry and thirsty; so often denied myself food, gone cold and naked. And all this, over and above something else which I do not count; I mean the burden I carry every day, my anxious care for all the churches" (2 Cor. 11. 27–28). Life is not an untroubled cruise, but a daily combat. . . .

In addition, whatever the apostle does with loving concern for the Kingdom helps to build up the Church. "Even as I write, I am glad of my sufferings on your behalf, as, in this mortal frame of mine, I help to pay off the debt which the afflictions of Christ still leave to be paid, for the sake of his body, the Church" (Col. 1. 24). And in this case also it is in order that life may abound that the Christian takes trials in his stride and does without. "We carry about continually in our bodies the dying state of Jesus, so that the living power of Jesus may be manifested in our bodies too" (2 Cor. 4. 10). And so joy and detachment come together. God loves a cheerful giver, and he makes this cheer brimful. It is the joy experienced by St Francis of Assisi singing the Canticle of Creation at a time when he had just received the stigmata of the Passion, when his sight was failing, when his companions were growing slack and his life was ending at forty, worn out in the service of Christ and his brethren. It was evangelical not worldly joy, the joy of the converted Christian who knows God.

CHAPTER IX

SIN: THE CONTRADICTION OF LIFE

We hear it said that for contemporary Christians, the young especially, the sense of sin has gone the same way as the sense of God. And it is indeed true that some of the directives of the moral conscience have been widely lost. These directives are those most in evidence in the past, for instance, submission to positive law (e.g. the commandments of the Church) and to the imperatives of sexual morality. On the other hand, it is only fair to note the acquisition of a more lively conscience in matters of social justice and charity. But perhaps the most instructive characteristic is the slight importance attached to sin, even when its distinctiveness as sin is understood. This is a normal accident of changing times and it is not unduly disturbing. We are a long way from those medieval Christians whom preachers could arouse to passionate repentance, who admitted their sins, went on pilgrimages and crusades for pardon. They sinned, but they knew it.

We may inquire, however, whether this sense of sin in our Christian ancestors was sufficiently critical and pure as to give them an idea of sin in accordance with the Gospel. Under slightly different forms in medieval popular religion and in Jansenism and Puritanism of the following centuries, it seems to have been sullied by fear and to some extent by Pharisaism. It is difficult to discern the exact truth of the intentions that lie behind religious behaviour, but the development of the modern conscience may have freed believers from certain feelings and instinctive reactions which were formerly confused with the expression of a Christian sense of sin.

When psychiatrists say that the idea of sin current in certain Christian circles creates morbid consequences and fosters neuroses, they are probably right. But is this idea, however widespread, more than a parody of the Christian notion of sinfulness? The same question arises when Maurice Boissais, in his novel, *Le goût du péché* (Julliard, 1954), describes the tragic story of young people, the victims of a puritan education over whose youth the terror of sin has brooded as the central reality of the Christian life. It does not seem to have been asked in the past.

There is, however, one certainty in Christian tradition as manifested by the saints: the sense of sin is the exact correlative of the sense of holiness. As they advanced in the holiness of Christ, so their consciousness of being sinners grew. Ordinary Christians might think they exaggerated, but it was no exhibition of humility: it was the truth about themselves as seen in the light of God's love. Sin has meaning only with reference to God, and a consciousness of sin is dependent upon the perception of God's glory as reflected in Christ. "Leave me to myself, Lord, he said; I am a sinner" (Luke 5. 8).

One of the tasks of the Christian education of conscience is to show how this authentic sense of sin may be gained. Its special character comes from its place in Christian life. Rather than moaning over the loss of a form which was not always genuine, we have something positive to do. If the sense of sin is correlative with that of holiness, then this gain will be progressive and be completed only in the adult. How in fact will the genesis of this sense take place at the different stages of the individual's growth? It is to this problem that we now turn.

TOWARDS A SENSE OF SIN

The moral conscience of the child is spontaneously objective: good and evil exist, together with their respective sanctions, the permitted and the forbidden absolutely fixed by laws and commandments. Breaking the rules means more to him than sin. The Christian child should not remain on this level, which he shares in common with almost every non-Christian child who is "well brought up".

How is the transition made from the notion of breaking rules to that of sin? By bringing in the God of Jesus Christ. Not only God as lawgiver and judge, but as the one who calls man to himself and gives him a new life, whose laws are not arbitrary and despotic, but the means of man's true development. His greatness lies in his fatherhood and his mercy.

It is because he is going to grow up that it is essential to Christianize the child's ideas of breaking rules. Sin as a contradiction of true life and an offence against Christ—that is an idea which, implanted in a child, can stand development. For once childhood is over the idea of breaking rules will be criticized and may then seem outmoded (unless, of course, childhood is unduly prolonged, creating a childish moral conscience with only legal sanctions that lasts on even when adult. This is a not infrequent occurrence and leads otherwise normal adults to mention in confession that they have touched the host with their teeth, or spoken bad words or contradicted their parents).

These examples also show the extreme care which teachers should take not to let the commandments which express God's will be confused with social customs. One may not use an alibi to get a child to allow its parents a few moments' peace.

With adolescence comes the uneasy conscience. The young man has discovered within himself ideals and exigencies, and his idea of sin refers to these rather than to extrinsic laws. His own feeling in fact would be expressed in terms of fault rather than sin, a fault against himself, his ideal, his code of honour; and this would be accompanied by shame, anger at obstacles, sometimes almost discouragement. It is a state that represents a growth of conscience, so long as he does not become a victim to it. This he would be if he let it become narcissistic, turning in on himself, becoming absorbed in his fault, or allowing his gloom to become despair.

Again at this stage the guilty conscience must be changed into an authentic consciousness of sin. There are three ways of doing this:

1. The adolescent can be led to see that his faith gives a meaning to his ideals, and shows them to be personal calls from Christ. He can be helped to be concerned not only with a subjective interest in himself but also with an objective interest in God and in Christ.

2. He can be given a wider moral ideal, not confined to the control of his emotions—especially sexual emotion—now beginning to develop. He should be taught to respond to universal love, to the world of God in Jesus Christ. The theme of his life should be self-giving and service for others. That will enable his emotions to develop on Christian lines.

3. He should be taught that divine forgiveness is not a pious sentiment, but a reality. Christ gives us a vision of sin that is parallel with the vision of holiness. But he does not let sin crush us: if our faith is serious he forgives. An adolescent tends to be subjective and sentimental. He must be taught to leave these attitudes behind. It is already an achievement if they are not encouraged, as it is all too easy to do.

Failure to take these steps is the reason why many remain permanently adolescent in their moral outlook. Sin is confused with subjective disgruntlement over faults, shame is confused with contrition. Sexual sins become an obsession. Or, on the other hand, supposed integrity becomes the subject of Pharisaical complacency. Worse than this is that unconscious morbidity to be found in many Christians which is the enemy of all authentic moral freedom and its exigencies.

SIN AND THE ADULT CHRISTIAN

You know well enough that when he was revealed to us, it was to take away our sins; there is no sinfulness in him, and no one can dwell in him and be a sinner. The sinner must be one who has failed to see him, failed to recognize him. Little children, do not allow anybody to mislead you; the man who lives right is the man who is right with God; he, too, is right in all his dealings. The man who lives sinfully takes his character from the devil; the devil was a sinner from the first. If the Son of God was revealed to us, it was so that he might undo what the devil had done, and if a man is born of God, he does not live sinfully, he is born to his parentage; he cannot be a sinner if he is born of God. This, then, is how God's children are known apart. A man cannot trace his origin from God if he does not live right, if he does not love his brethren (1 John 3. 5–10).

These words of St John take us to the heart of the Christian conception of sin. We will consider their main ideas.

The sinner has not seen or recognized Jesus Christ. Sin, therefore, is to be understood with reference to our relationship with Christ, and as an act of personal disloyalty. Every sin is a deed done against faith (in the biblical sense) in Jesus Christ. It indicates lack of attention, heedlessness, pushing on one side.

If a man is born of God he cannot sin because the divine life is developing in him. St John is describing the normal logic of life in Christ which is the development of a divine principle (the Holy Spirit, supernatural consciousness) embracing the whole of life and every aspect of experience in the man who has received it by faith in Christ. Sin is out of step with God's universal plan and with the world being formed by the total Christ, Christ and all his members.

Sin contradicts existence as a child of God, practising holiness, imitating Christ, loving the brethren. It is not simply a matter of going against laws, even divine ones, or against ideals, however noble. To understand sin involves the realization that God is holy, that Christ is holy, that the Christian is called to the holiness of God through the imitation of Christ.

So when I sin I go counter to the direction of the Spirit within me and to the following of Christ which should be my way. I act against my own interest inasmuch as I oppose God's plan for me, and against his universal purpose into which my whole life should enter. The commandments I kept as a child, the inner calling I heard as a youth, these were but partial expressions of the Christian vocation which makes ever-increasing demands upon me and takes every detail of my conduct into its orbit. Unless we have experienced the infinite attraction of deeper and deeper communion with Christ, the mediator of God's holiness, we have not understood the nature of sin. "In the Lord you are all daylight. You must live as men native to the light . . . your lives must be the manifestation of God's will. As for the thankless deeds men do in the dark, you must not take part in them" (Ephes. 5. 8–11).

SIN AND SINS

For this reason the classification of sins by the criterion of the commandments alone serves as a starting point, but must be quickly left behind. Then questions such as the following have to be asked: Have I sinned by omission? Am I complacently content with the absolute minimum to keep my conscience quiet? If so, it shows that I am more concerned with respectability than with responding to the summons of Christ. When sin is really understood three results follow:

1. The distinction between precepts and counsels is merely pedagogic. Christ demands that I should spend myself to the limit—and this is in accordance with the precepts. But it goes beyond their simple application and falls under the constant motivation of the counsels of holiness. It increas-

ingly demands actions in imitation of Christ which do not come within the scope of the precepts considered statically.

2. The gravity of a sin will be measured by the extent in which it acts against holy living. Something which centrally disturbs our union with Christ is infinitely more serious than what affects whatever is only externally related to Christ. Examination of conscience must be made with reference to Christ and to holiness, and not to ethical, social or psychological values only.

3. The realm of Christ's holiness is progressively discovered by the Christian. Sensitivity to sin grows parallel with life in Christ. Like human love, divine love grows in intensity, in mutual demands, and in mutual understanding. That which, at a given stage, is not perceived to be a grave sin, is realized to be so later. The moral conscience develops by degrees, and even earnest Christians only realize gradually the objective demands of holiness. Not to refuse the day's demands—that is the request made to everyone, and to seek a more perfect imitation of Christ, especially through that fraternal love which is its quintessence: "As God's favoured children, you must be like him. Order your lives in charity, upon the model of that charity which Christ showed us, when he gave himself up on our behalf" (Ephes. 5. 1–2).

SIN: CONTRITION: FREEDOM FROM SIN

A Christian, unlike Puritans of all types, is not interested in sin for its own sake. He looks at it from God's and Christ's point of view. That is what we have tried to show. There is, however, one thing more. God and his Christ forgive sin. *Credo in remissionem peccatorum.* Christ has freed us from the unresolved anguish of sin. Divine forgiveness has certain bearings upon the adult Christian consciousness of sin:

1. First, as regards contrition. This is only possible for a believer, for it is quite different from personal or social shame, wounded self-love, or discouragement. An adolescent finds it hard to make the right distinctions. "I (the prodigal

son) will arise and go to my father and say to him, Father, I have sinned against heaven and before thee" (Luke 15. 17). That is contrition; a judgement about a disordered situation made by the light of faith, a repudiation of this disorder and a decision to return to absolute fidelity to Christ. The Holy Spirit may give the grace of physical sadness and the gift of tears to the contrite sinner. But this supernatural accompaniment should not be confused with natural emotion or anguish which depend upon age and temperament. It is an illuminating fact that the gravest spiritual sins rarely cause shame or anguish.

2. As regards confession. It is not a rite which provides compensation—a kind of electric shock—for the legalist conscience so that it can come into line again or for the morbid conscience to regain peace. It is Christ's word that matters. The sinner believes that this word avails to create a new heart in him, so long as he acts with integrity and enters into the rite with his whole personality. It is not a magical, but a sacramental rite.

3. It follows that we must distinguish the peace of forgiveness in Christ from the purely psychological feeling of comfort. In American factories "lay confessors" have been installed to increase output by simply listening to employees burdened with anxiety. The sacrament of penance is not a psychiatric cure, and its merely human effect in bringing peace of mind should not be emphasized in its defence. Here again the reference is to God and Christ. The Holy Spirit may indeed give a supernatural experience of peace, but the certitude and the reality lie in the word of forgiveness, in independence of that experience. A purely psychological feeling of deliverance is limited by the same factors that we noted with regard to anguish and shame.

The sense of sin is relative to the sense of holiness; and for contemporary Christians the regaining of an authentic sense of sin, in the spirit of the prophets and the Gospel, depends upon the measure of their response to the call to sanctity.

CHAPTER X

THE CHRISTIAN, THE MOST RESPONSIBLE OF MEN

Non-Christians sometimes say that Christians are lacking in a sense of responsibility. This may sound somewhat astonishing after our inquiry into the roots of Christian living has shown the gravity of every Christian act, the seriousness of all use of the freedom given to man by God. To be irresponsible means that one lacks the strength to answer to oneself, to other men and to God for one's actions, or that one lacks even the idea that one ought to answer for them. The life work of a Christian consists in doing his utmost for the glory of God. Therefore the witnesses answering for each moment of his life will be his own conscience, the constant alerting of that conscience by his relations with his brethren and with God and God's plan for the history of the world.

It is obvious therefore that the charge is not valid against authentic Christian conduct. But it is not made in bad faith when it envisages false forms of that conduct. If a Christian, unworthy of his calling, confines himself to mere respectability he will hardly bother about answering for his life either to his own conscience or to others, even if he holds to the distant prospect of answering after death to God. If he tends more to the spirituality of the sage than to specifically Christian morality the failure to accept responsibility for his concrete actions means that individualism is close at hand.

We may benefit therefore from a consideration of responsibility as a fundamental quality of Christian conduct. It will complete that return to Christian sources which has been attempted in the previous chapters and make use of the directives there discovered.

No one, in fact, is so responsible as a Christian man.

THE CHRISTIAN RESPONSIBLE THROUGH HIS CONSCIENCE AND HIS LIFE

As a Christian my responsibility for every one of my deeds must show itself first of all in my conscience and my life. My conscience becomes responsible as soon as it makes a decision and commits itself. My life must show responsibility because no moment of it as a Christian can be isolated from the whole of which it forms an active part, any more than the thread can be divorced from the tapestry it is helping to weave.

The responsibility of conscience

A responsible conscience presupposes a profound appreciation of human decision. Our world has become extraordinarily complicated as a result of technical specialization and world-wide pressures which influence the most personal elements of our being. Amidst these difficulties and because of them a Christian needs more than ever an understanding of decisive choice.

We may ask: "How can I know what Christ wants me to do?" It is a sensible question. On the one hand, I find myself in a given human situation; it is unique and like no other; it occurs in a given place and at a given point in time. I come to it accompanied by whatever factors are psychologically determined in me, with my temperament and education. My personality as a whole is involved in the complexity of the historical situation. On the other hand, I am in organic unity with the living Christ, in contact by faith with his divine and human vitality. And through this situation a summons from Christ reaches me, asking me to lift it, by faith, into the Christosphere. Christ calls and I must answer. This is what is involved in the question: "How can I know with as much certainty as possible what Christ wants me to do here and now?" A very general answer can be given at once: it is by entering into the human situation with the utmost integrity, and at the same time renewing the vital energy of my faith in Christ.

Who will make the synthesis between the human situation and faith? To take an example: who must make the synthesis of all the concrete data of a given passion of human love in which I am involved and what Christ wants to be done with this passion? It is I myself and no one else. For this vital synthesis which must have a decisive choice as its outcome, can only be made in one laboratory: my conscience vivified by grace. Certainly I should take advice and also see what bearing the traditional Christian solution of moral problems, discussed above, may have upon my synthesis. But this tradition cannot produce a ready-made, final and concrete solution to my question, even supposing that its catalogue contains a case that is really identical in every aspect with mine. And it has to be noted also that as a result of the speed of historical and moral evolution during the last decades it is not likely that tradition will be more than approximately helpful, although always of value. For contemporary Christians the addition of creative imagination springing from the life of faith is absolutely necessary. And the difficulty should not be side-tracked by appealing to authority or to a spiritual director to settle it for me. It is I who am questioned by Christ at this moment of my life, and it is I who must answer, without shirking my responsibility.

It is no use pretending that Christian conduct does not always involve some risk, a risk that may occasionally lead to error. Catholic moral tradition unanimously agrees that the erroneous conscience must be followed. Of course every precaution to avoid error must be taken, but even then it is not always possible to do so. And in the tragic alternative of a conflict of duties, the risk lies in having failed to choose the duty that was in reality essential. But risk must not frighten us; for life always involves risk. We must come to a decision and act. If we systematically refuse to face certain issues under cover of the precept—too widely interpreted—that requires flight from occasions of sin; if we therefore abstain from acting and neutralize conflicts which are the normal outcome of the complexity of life, it is an indication of our spinelessness and the reason why we are moral absentees and sinners by omission. Many a Christian is afraid of life and freedom. Christ does not want the obedience of a slave from us. We can never have a conscience that is too free, too enlightened or too personal, whether we are concerned with an act of faith or with Christian conduct in general.

The responsibility of my whole life

On the other hand what indeed might give us cause to fear, if we paid sufficient attention to it, is the reflection that each decisive choice made by me has a universal repercussion for good or evil over my whole life so long as it lasts. The total unity of the living being is repeated in each of its elementary tissues, and in a similar way each responsible act of ours contains within it the totality of our existence as moral persons. Spiritually, man is a much more sensitive being than we commonly imagine.

As examples of this truth we may consider the following: A Christian, having reached the age of responsible choice, has refused to commit his life to a path which would involve a more wholehearted generosity—e.g. he has refused the priestly or monastic calling, made an ill-considered marriage, chosen a job for its money alone. By this initial betrayal of integrity he will have freely let loose a kind of fatality that will weigh upon his life. It is at least a very serious hypothesis.

When we come up against temptation are we not what we have made ourselves, weak as a result of every act of cowardice, strong from every deed done in the truth? Sometimes we genuinely think that we cannot fulfil certain obligations which concern a whole section of our life. May we not often find ourselves responsible for thus having to break with them? Maybe we took them on too lightly, or having taken them on, led such a distracted life that gradually they have ceased to have any meaning for us. How can we hope to retain any fervour in life so long as we "sadden the Holy Spirit" within us? To pass by on the other side, when we are called to some heroic deed of fraternal charity or purity, is not done without payment.

There is a contemporary trend of thought, called personalist, which insists with the utmost emphasis on the gravity of decisive choice and on the risks involved in human moral action. The more we agree with this, the less acceptable will the conclusions be which the existentialists draw from it. These latter hold that actions simply follow one another without continuity, their value coming solely from the sincerity and clear-sightedness with which they originated. The moral conscience, they say, is the source of decision, but not in any sense as a permanent illumination. The moral life is not an embryo consistently developing, taking the past into the future and the future into the present. As Christians we have a nobler responsibility, and one that is less nerve-racking because it is based on hope, on God's faithfulness which asks for ours, so that we may become holy and that God's Kingdom may come.

This then is the justification of Christian responsibility on the personal plane. It demands that we consider very seriously what we do—although not tensely and drearily—especially when it is a question of those more important decisions that will produce an effect on life for a long time to come. We shall find that our freedom—so entangled with non-freedom in our daily life—will deepen its channel considerably at such times of decisive choice. Every man, however pathological, has certain moments when he can use his freedom to say yes or no with incalculable consequences. Do those concerned with Christian education pay sufficient attention to this fact?

THE CHRISTIAN'S SOCIAL RESPONSIBILITY

Christian conduct involves personal sanctification and responsibility. But it is also and necessarily acted out within the Church; it is holiness within a mystical Body. And this opens out a new dimension for Christian responsibility; the consequences of what a Christian man does affects in every way far more than his individual life. By "in every way" we mean first the community of Christians and then the community of all men. For all mankind and the whole of human history acquire their full meaning in the mystical Body of Christ.

In the Christian community

Do Christians normally realize the consequences that flow from the dogma of the communion of saints? For these would make them conscious that they are truly responsible for the Christian life of their brethren and that they are ontologically involved in it. In some Christian parishes it would seem that this consciousness of solidarity only rises to the surface when a scandal occurs. And then if one is a member of the unsmirched section of the flock, what an invitation to Pharisaic behaviour that is!

Each single member of a Christian community must integrate the communal dimension into his behaviour. When I am trying to find out what Christ wants me to do I must leave room for what the Church wants me to do. Is this deed likely to cause scandal rather than "build up"; if it is then I must keep off it, unless indeed it is only the Pharisees who will be shocked. When a man falls, who is to say that they are not responsible for his fall, if they had done nothing to hold him up before he fell? It is untrue to say that such a matter is no concern of ours, even though the assumption of responsibility for it may sometimes require much tact.

In the community of mankind

This demands reflection on what the collective effect of personal conduct and the political dimension of human activity should make a Christian do.

"Christians, as such, play no part in politics", that was a slogan that influenced many Christians during the first quarter of this century. Cardinal Suhard was fond of relating a conversation he had had with Pius XII. The pope had insisted that Catholics should pay much more serious attention to political affairs from the point of view of moral education and apostolic testimony. Cardinal Suhard agreed, but recalled the discredit which the word "political" carried with it for French Catholics, to whom in fact politics had done much harm, and he suggested that it would be better to speak of education in citizenship. "If you like, and in order to avoid misunderstanding," replied Pius XII, "but the real word is political." It is a story that tells much, for it is only too true that until recently to a Catholic the word "politics" evoked a world in which ambition, cunning, oratorical humbug, foregone conclusions, half-truths, promptly submerged the conscience of even the most honest. And to this was added the memory of political conflicts in which during the nineteenth century the Church of France lost the better part of her strength and compromised her spiritual credit by injudiciously taking sides. The reaction against politics that had become a routine without conscience, as well as against "political Catholicism", was a salutary experience. But its lessons would have been missed if they were taken as commending a contemptuous indifference to the realities with which politics are concerned, to political responsibility and to the activities relating to it.

> It is a difficult and indispensable task [remarked Cardinal Feltin recently] which Christians must confront as a duty they have disregarded and whose existence, even, many of them hardly suspect. Because they have been rightly warned against political passion which leads to anarchy or against those compromises which tempt men of power, some Catholics

have for too long ignored, denigrated or run away from
political tasks and have abstained from them under the pretext
of keeping to the spirit of the Gospel, as though Christ had
not commanded what is due to Caesar must be rendered to
Caesar (*Pax Christi*, Assisi, September 9th, 1952).

What then is the reality that underlies politics? It is the
synthesis of the issues that arise from the universal inter-
relationships of the things that bind mankind into a common
destiny. It is the domain in which the physical, economic,
technical and cultural spheres are coordinated in view of an
increasingly unified world in which each person and every
community shall find an opportunity for human advancement. Political reality comes into being so soon as there is a
common good to be served and a human community—a
family, tribe, city, social group or nation—to be advanced
in the direction of personal freedom. But today it cannot be
confined to the family, social or civic stages. To try to do this
is the temptation of those who are frightened of politics and
who say they will keep to non-political family, social or civic
development. For the forms which the administration of the
common good of mankind has taken, over the ages and
according to the progressive rhythm of history, have constantly grown bigger, from the Greek city states up to modern
nations and federations—to mention only the West.

To disregard history is to narrow our vision of the world.
A similar narrowing occurs if we forget the common good of
mankind and refuse to subscribe to a political reality which
shall unite men above and beyond family relationships,
economic interests, social solidarities, geographical neigh-
bourhood and cultural community. The world that has come
out of the industrial and technical revolutions has developed
the universal interdependence of human collectivities, and
democratic consciousness calls each and every one to take
part in that administration of the common good which
formerly belonged to rulers alone. Political reality has gained
in expansion and depth. A man today is only really adult
if he shares this outlook of universal dependence and of

universal social intercourse, if he makes an effort to come into the construction that contains mankind as a whole and determines the real history of all its lesser groups. Too many remain immature, swamped and lost in a world that has grown too big for them, unable to see what is happening in the context of the whole.

If we want a political conscience we must first become aware in a vital and considered way of the political reality as it is in the present stage of the world's evolution. Obviously it is not by cutting ourselves off from it, by turning inwards on ourselves or our particular social group that we shall succeed in acquiring this conscience. Today, whether we like it or not, every particular event has a political dimension. Neither the proud and aloof, nor those concerned only with doing things, nor the cynical, from all of whom a basic political conscience is absent, can exercise valid political action bearing upon the decisive factors of mankind's common good. Nor can those men who profess to trust in providence but who refuse to enter the stream of the real movement of technical, economic and social advance.

Charity is political

"The domain of politics," said Pius XI, "which concerns the interests of society as a whole, is the field of the widest charity, of political charity, of which it may be said that there is none above it, save that of religion" (Discourse to the Catholic Federation of the Italian Universities, December 18th, 1927).

If we take our stand on the Christian plane, it is clear that the conscience and the life of men who are animated by faith must take on this political dimension of human life. The Kingdom of God is entangled with man and with human history in their complete reality.

The Gospel as a living organism has no difficulty in adopting this political development of the life and events of contemporary man. Already, beforehand, it is open to every call for more unity and universality. Always, beforehand, it breathes the spirit of disinterestedness and of service on a collective plane, of love for the poorest and for the victims of the great powers of egoism. Christians should have less difficulty than others in accepting the promotion of under-developed peoples, the disinterestedness of the developed nations and the condemnation of nationalism, the fight against the rule of money and of private interests. They ought to be the first to raise their charity to the sphere of the general causes of social injustice. Charity makes wider demands than in the past and can no longer be satisfied with personal relations. Less than ever can the Christian realist content himself with strictly but narrowly fulfilling the duties of his position in life.

On all hands the personal responsibility of every Christian is being urged to widen out to the dimensions of the mystical Body. As each day passes the universal solidarity of all men becomes less and less an abstraction. All the facts—econo-mic, political, military—make this abundantly plain. Whether we realize it or not, no one of our actions, however personal it may be, can keep clear of this new network of human communion, for their responsibility is extending ever more widely. If we realize that the half-dead man helped by the Good Samaritan is today represented by a thousand million men, under-nourished, ill-housed, under-educated—four-fifths of mankind—does this not at least dictate a deepening of the Christian outlook on material goods and the fight for social justice? All things press me with the question of the coming of others upon the scene, whether these are near or far, and I cannot shirk the answer.

Collectivization and technical civilization modify the social conditions of human life. It is rarely in my power to give a direction to destructive factors that have come into existence as a result of historical development. But it is my duty to work with Christians and non-Christians for the production of a moral conscience and for the means of influence whereby it can be effective, adapted to the present requisites for peace and for international and social justice, and to what is sound in the contemporary outlook. The task may be beyond us; but that does not do away with our solidarity with a civilization that is coming to be, in its encounter with the spirit of the Gospel. Terrible in this respect is the responsibility of Christians who are in positions of social command; the consequences of an omission, of a compromise on their part, may be incalculable. But each of us in our daily life affects the Kingdom of God as it exists in the historical present and all mankind also, far more often than we imagine.

The most fatal attitude would be to excuse ourselves under the pretext that we were not up to date and have not seen what goes on around us, whereas faith makes it a duty that we should face up to the world in which we live and understand the problems it raises for the practice of Christian charity.

These perspectives of Christian responsibility are upsetting for complacent peace and illusory moral security. Of course our responsibility raises issues beyond our power. Christ alone can measure and judge it. When we have done our utmost, the uncertainty of our conscience will not fail to be a torment. It is then that we should turn to him who one day will judge the world and history: it is he who is our judge from now onwards. It is a certainty that brings peace to a troubled conscience. This peace does not mean that we have given up the job, but that we trust Christ wholly, and hence it is a peace we can accept.

For myself, I make little account of your scrutiny, or of any human audit-day; I am not even at pains to scrutinize my own conduct. My conscience does not, in fact, reproach me; but that is not where my justification lies; it is the Lord's scrutiny I must undergo. You do ill, therefore, to pass judgement prematurely, before the Lord's coming; he will bring to light what is hidden in darkness, and reveal the secrets of men's hearts; then each of us will receive his due award from God (1 Cor. 4. 2–5).

CHAPTER XI

THE CHRISTIAN: IN THE WORLD, BUT NOT OF IT

The Christian movement is in the world and traverses it. Its mission is to be the world's leaven. What then will be the relation between the Christian and this world?

Our minds may turn at once to those Christians who are monks and priests whose lives, in different ways, indicate a break with the world. But these are specialized Christians whose vocation or functions leads them to emphasize a position of standing back from the world. The monk does so in order to testify that the Kingdom is already in the world; the priest, in order to testify that the Kingdom is primarily established from above. The separation from the world differs in meaning and form in the case of the monk and that of the priest. What is the position of those other Christians who are in the world, but not of it?

An anonymous Christian author of the second century explains this relationship in a letter to a pagan describing Christianity to him:

> Christians are not marked off from other men by their country, their language or their clothes. They do not live in special towns, or use an unusual dialect; there is nothing peculiar about their way of life.... They are spread out among the Greek and barbarian cities according as their lot has settled them; they conform to local usage in clothes, food and way of life, whilst at the same time displaying the extraordinary and truly paradoxical laws of their own way

of life. Each lives in his native country, but as a foreigner domiciled in it. Every foreign country is a homeland to them, and their homeland is foreign. They are in the flesh, but do not live by its laws. They pass their life on earth, but are citizens of heaven. . . . In a word, what the soul is in the body, Christians are in the world (*Letter to Diognetus*, Chapter 5).

It is therefore an old problem, looked at already from every angle, but not yet exhausted. It will remain a contemporary problem until the world ends, without a final solution. Every adult Christian needs to reflect on it. What does temporal activity entail for a disciple of Christ? What part should he take in the work of man in history, from the economic to the cultural sphere, in everything covered by the word civilization? What will be the attitude of one who believes in heaven, of the saint, in face of all man's efforts to organize, improve, and transform the earth's surface from generation to generation? Will it be indifference, evasion, resigned consent or passionate commitment?

THE PRIMACY OF THE KINGDOM OF GOD

The words of the Gospel come to mind: "How is a man the better for it, if he gains the whole world at the cost of losing his own soul?" (Matt. 16. 26). And also St Paul's words: "Only, brethren, I would say this; the time is drawing to an end; nothing remains, but for those who have wives to behave as though they had none; those who weep must forget their tears, and those who rejoice their rejoicing, and those who buy most renounce possession; and those who take advantage of what the world offers must not take full advantage of it; the fashion of this world is soon to pass away" (1 Cor. 7. 29–32). These revealed texts give us a straight answer: the Kingdom of God is here; the world and human history have lost the point of their development, do not delay over them; Christian grace alone counts.

We feel instinctively—not simply because our self-giving to God is half-hearted but in the name of the authentic

Christian experience of the whole Church—that this way of acting would be too simple to serve as an expression of all God wants with regard to the present world.

And yet what these words say is the heart of the matter: the created world and human history do not contain in their own resources the hope and the power of conclusive salvation. The first Christian generation has forcefully handed down to us its conviction about the primacy of the Kingdom founded by the Lord Jesus: "I am Alpha, I am Omega ... he who is and ever was, and is still to come ... who rules over earthly kings" (Apoc. 1. 8 and 5). It is true that this Kingdom was established in a world that pre-exists to ours, but what matters is not so much its continuity with this pre-existent world as the fact that through God's intervention it is a novelty in ours; the interest lies in its inauguration here by God and not in any expansion it might gain through human effort. Besides there is no more time, and no one is interested in promoting historical growth because history ended with the events of Easter and Pentecost and the world is in a state of suspension until all men shall have been enabled to receive the extraordinary news of their call to the Kingdom and until the Lord returns.

The early Christians therefore could not find anything in their experience which committed them to positive temporal works in the name of Christ (here is meant, of course, something more than the minimum necessary for personal and social subsistence, regarded as provisional, and as a charitable care for the daily needs of their brethren). There is no Manicheism in this attitude; the world is not evil, it only lacks stability. Nothing is so human as the Gospel. It simply means that the only point of the present world is to be of service in the new creation in Jesus Christ.

It is good for twentieth-century Christians that the Christian position was given this stamp of the primacy of the Kingdom from the start. The problems of our life as Christians are more complex than these early brethren could have imagined. And this has come about because history continues to unfold its earthly course. But the essential notes remain as data: salvation comes from Jesus Christ; the whole course of history is already judged by Jesus Christ who is its invisible Lord. When the Kingdom is completed we shall see that all things are held together in Christ; the achievement of history will finally be the achievement of sanctity, of the love of Christ and the welcome given him. This is expressed by Pascal:

> Jesus Christ, without possessions, without producing anything, exists in his sphere of holiness. He left no inventions, he did not reign; but he was patient, holy, holy with God's holiness, terrible to the demons, without sin of any kind.... It would have been useless for our Lord Jesus Christ to come as king in order to dazzle in his reign of holiness, but in his own sphere he did come dazzlingly (*Pensées*, 793).

MISSIONARY RELATIONSHIP WITH THE WORLD

An immediate result of this primacy of the Kingdom affects the lives of Christians directly; like that of the Church, their life can ultimately be nothing but missionary. This epithet is not meant to summon up ideas of conquest, aggression, the will to force one's convictions or to flag-wave for one's own Church. The missionary idea is very different from proselytism; it begins by leaving self behind. It is not a question of one's own ideas, generosity or militant temperament, but of those of Christianity whose initial suppositions by their nature concern all men, and so must spread in the world and gain publicity. It is the Church's task to make them visible and attractive in the world. It is the Church's task and the task of every member of the Church so to work that grace and the Gospel may be brought to those who still do not know Christ. Christian hope must become more widespread for the glory of God and the life of the world.

With such convictions a Christian is bound to be a missionary. He cannot live in Christ and not share Christ and collaborate in the extension of his reign. Missionary action takes many forms according to circumstances and vocations; its essence does not lie in forms—provided these are valid and genuine—but in the quality of the relation established with the world in the name of Christ. Here less than any-where is there room for trickery, for God always advances in the open.

HOW HUMAN HISTORY COLLABORATES IN THE KINGDOM

Should all Christians become monks or missionaries? If the primitive Christian position were complete, and putting the actual condition of the world on one side, then they should. In any case we can understand why some Christians do choose the monastic vocation: they remind us of those essential things which we might forget or attenuate. But in spite of the spiritual event which, in Jesus Christ, stamped it with its final destiny, the world continues to turn; mankind develops demographically; economic needs increase; the "long revolution" of the masses into the common culture is slowly coming about; political relations embrace increasingly vast areas. In the midst of this evolution in history, man is in labour, a human spirituality is at work. The width and depth of temporal action are both extending.

It gives definition to the theoretical question: what is the relation between the order of holiness and the order of civilization? The latter is a fact; it cannot be denied or declared unequivocally hostile to the order of holiness. In any case the Church has assisted its development consider-ably. Nor can she be indifferent, for it concerns man, and the Kingdom subjects the whole man and his real life to herself.

"Separated from me, you have no power to do anything" (John 15. 5). Nothing that is merely human will be immortal-ized in the Kingdom. You may experience human beauty, dominate the physical universe, and to some extent practise social justice and enjoy human love, but death and pre-cariousness are bound up with all these achievements which belong to this earth only. On the other hand, when creation comes finally to glory, Christ will appear as the author of the universal triumph. Is it not therefore certain that then everything that through man's freedom has come to accept Christ and to collaborate in the Kingdom will be made manifest? So that the more human values—the development of conscience, the control of instinct, creative expression, mastery of the world and fraternity—are put under Christ's rule, the more striking will be the world's permanence in God. "The nations will live and move in the light of the Lamb, and the kings of the earth will bring it their tribute of praise and honour" (Apoc. 21. 24–26). The Kingdom is a kingdom of men living in all the dimensions of mankind and Christ leaves nothing that is attached to man on one side, provided that man is attached to him. It is a question of the conversion of the world through the conversion of man. The order of civilization now re-enters into the orbit of the order of holiness. And that in a twofold way.

Human history prepares its content for the Kingdom

When Revelation speaks of a "new heaven and a new earth", it enables us to affirm that it is the first creation in its totality, together with all the historical development which man shall have effected in it which, in God's purpose, must be recapitulated in Jesus Christ. And this gives the dimensions of the catholicity of the Church in which all human values converted to Christ are to be found, so that God may receive the glory of them and that the glory of God may transfigure them. For it is everything that has been offered to God that will finally become the reality of the second creation in Jesus Christ. It is obvious, however, that it is man and his heart, coming before material things and technical conquests, who is the first candidate for the Kingdom and, in dependence on the community of persons, the whole world of historical happenings. History constitutes, day after day, that which will be saved: the stones of the City of God.

Human history is the substratum of the Kingdom

It is within definite historical situations that the events of sacred history occur and that the Kingdom grows. These situations may offer favourable or unfavourable conditions, occasions that open out to the grace of the Kingdom or occasions when the material organization of human society closes it to the Kingdom. Civilization's reference to the Kingdom, in this case, is more external than in its previously mentioned function, but it is still capital and encourages us to act in history.

How does Christ reign effectively over human history? The answer can be given with certainty. It is through the mediations which he has left to his Church and which ensures the presence and power of the risen Lord among believers. This is not guesswork; Christ himself foresaw the way in which he would continue his Incarnation and his Passover among us. And through us: for Christians, as Christ's instruments, become the means by which all the elements of history enter his vivifying influence. It is through us, through our faith, through our perpetual Eucharist in union with that of Christ, through the activity of our prayer and our contemplation that human history becomes sacred history in reality.

In the Church and through faith in Christ the course of history enters into the stream of Christian development and is thus directed to its eternal consecration. But what are we to say of so many elements in history—and among them the amplest and richest—that have not known their own meaning in the light of Christ? Will historical periods that have not discovered the means of their salvation in Christ be condemned? We should not make rash generalizations and go against God's universal plan of love for our world, a design that absorbs sin itself.

Apart from Christ history cannot transcend itself by the aid of its own resources alone. There is no infallible salvation in the elements of the world and history considered in themselves. Where salvation is concerned Christ cannot be shelved. And this means—it is a tragic conclusion that yet strengthens faith—that when human history deliberately refuses Christ by affirming its idolatry, and human values proclaim their self-sufficiency, their avarice and pride, it all seems utterly alien to the history of salvation.

But is there not a way, personal and collective, of being united to Christ, of accepting something of his sovereignty, apart from any explicit knowledge of his Revelation? There is. It is a genuine human love, the capacity of the human heart for offering. It is my conviction that human love is the salvation of wide areas of human history; that it constitutes the mediation which subjects human lives to Christ without their knowing it, together with such history as is bound up with them. Love bestows meaning upon all partial values, all techniques, all materials and cultural progress. If love has exorcized egoism it cannot come from Satan; for then it is Christ's. Love is the opposite of self-sufficiency and pride; it is a gift and every gift is related to God. If explicit Christian faith animates few things in human history Christ's power is not so closely bound up with it as might at first appear. In this respect does it not sometimes happen that the "world" is in the Church, whereas the Kingdom often animates— although only partially—that which visibly is outside the Church?

In any case, Christ abides as the leaven of history. His eternal youth abides when it grows old, just as in its inspired and creative periods. Mankind must be converted in order that human values may become realities of sacred history in Christ. In the contemporary world there are many moves towards love and peace from what may be called pre-Christian values looking for conversion to Christ who is as yet unknown or misunderstood.

We should have the clearsightedness to avoid both a false transcendence and a false incarnation: an incarnation in which there is no question of history being deified or of its entry into the order of the holy; a transcendence which is not worried at seeing practically all history moving to an end without meaning.

What does this need for clearsightedness entail for Christian conduct?

THE CHRISTIAN IN THE WORLD: COMMITTED AND UNCOMMITTED

We well know where false transcendence leads: to escapism, a flight to an "ideal" world and idleness. Right from the start St Paul had to correct the conduct of Christians who drew from the expectation of Christ's speedy return the conclusion that temporal duties could be neglected (cf. 2 Thess. 3). In more subtle forms many contemporary Christians with a somewhat abstract faith mistrust temporal commitments in which they fear that their heart as well as their faith will be compromised.

The opposite intention—that which follows upon a false idea of the Incarnation—is more generous, but quite as serious. It leads to the endowment of temporal movements with a Messianic significance, to the various forms of secularized Christianity, to embroilment in soulless agitation. It calls for a considered reaction on our part. We do not choose to be either committed or uncommitted in the world, although, within the unity of the Body of Christ, particular vocations may stress one point rather than another. It is a matter of tension; and the tension can be strong enough, according to circumstances and within the confines of Christian loyalty, to shift first to one pole and then to the other, from, say, the position of Christian social life in the world to that of the monastic life.

The Christian uncommitted

From every point of view the primary factor in our conduct belongs to faith in Christ. It is to him that we must first bind ourselves, to the divine pioneer of human history, if we want to exist and to act in the stream of sacred history.

Some Christians seem to be ashamed of what is stable, final, eschatologically absolute in our faith. It seems to them an anomaly in a world of restless inquiry, in whose history hope and despair exist together. They think that if they had not its key in Christ they would be closer to their time. They fear that their assurance, confirmed by the certitude of eternity, their joy, springing from the risen Lord, may harshly jar upon the wretchedness of real life. It is an attitude of integrity, seeking solidarity with mankind's lot. All the same, faith in Christ is not a form of wealth which, like human wealth, we can give up in order to become acceptable in certain sections of society. What should make us ashamed is the way we live from this faith, the spectacle we present to a world that expects something different from us than words and excommunications.

We do not look for any event that will be so capital and decisive for the collective and personal destiny of men as was the event of Jesus Christ. It will not be transcended.

We enter into reality, first, by allowing our present faith and worship to come under the influence of his death and resurrection. As always the contemplatives are right.

We can take a step further. Amidst the great wealth of values in the world today, some words of our Lord become paradoxically relevant: "If any one comes to me and does not hate [i.e. give less love to] his father, mother, wife, children, brothers and sisters, and even his own life, he cannot be my disciple." "Have no anxiety about the things of this world." "What does it avail for a man to gain the whole world, if the cost is his own life?"

Obviously we must become detached if we want to be one with Christ and to make him present in history. The material development of our time is ambiguous: one of its effects is to render the temptations of Jesus at the start of his public life an actuality for ourselves. Are we ready to reply to the solicitations of comfort and pleasure: "Man does not live by bread alone, but by every word that comes out of the mouth of God"? Are we ready to reply to the intoxication of power that surges around us: "Thou shalt worship the Lord thy God and him only shalt thou serve"? Without vigilance amidst the environing paganism, faith's vision of Christ grows unreal; he ceases to rise above the processes and powers of history; his transcendence is compromised.

To the young the cause of history and the ages of human creativity must continue with an inevitable logic. But in reality the present age of the world, like our own bodily life, must come to an end: "You are keeping it clearly in mind ... that the day of the Lord will come like a thief in the night. It is just when men are saying, All quiet, all safe, that doom will fall on them suddenly, like the pangs that come to a woman in travail" (1 Thess. 5. 2–3).

The Christian committed

And yet this world of well defined boundaries and this course of historical time that passes away form the arena of Christian hope because when Christ rose he carried them fundamentally into his glory. In union with Christ, his glory in contact with our mortality, we are compelled to remain in history not as resigned spectators but as active participants. In fact we have become an element of Christ in the world and his mystery constantly illuminates the meaning of its evolution. Whatever pertains to mankind gets its meaning from him.

Sloth then is out of the question. The work of the Christian in time, and its relation to historical development, does not simply provide him with an opportunity for practising professional duties and moral virtues, ignoring the objective worth of human achievement as something outside the Kingdom. Since the Christian's belief affects the world of his life this achievement is an integral part of the Kingdom. In working for it, the Christian collaborates in the Kingdom, but less directly than in the specific work of the Church. All the same he does bear responsibility for it, because the salvation of Christ not only penetrates into history, but participates in its activity. It is fundamentally realist and it makes the believer look at the world from a double angle—the world as it is, and as it is developing.

There are three motives, most often conjoined, which rouse a Christian to activity in the world:

The missionary motive

We are better acquainted than formerly with the real conditions requisite for persons and communities to draw near to faith. They are conditions of culture, sociology and history, the strata that affect freedom when it chooses faith. Not only individuals, but civilizations present themselves for the Gospel. Christians have a collective responsibility for the receptivity of the insulated condition of human communities.

Moreover, the more developed a man is, the more his awareness helps his freedom and gives him a conscientious and critical sense of his own existence, the more chance he has of a really personal faith. Christians ought not to be afraid of this development, as if it worked against religious tradition; they should be glad to have a share in a world in which men may play a personal part and have a faith that is less atavistic and more genuine. The Kingdom of Christ is not a collection of sub-men.

The motive of fraternal charity

This now means a charity that extends to the ends of the earth and makes use of institutions that are adapted to work in social and political spheres. The development of the modern world opens up a new field to charity where it may prove more effective than in the early centuries of Christianity. We are more alive to the fact that there are undeveloped, ill-housed, under-nourished countries and that the egoism of nations is more terrible than that of limited individual groups. For twentieth-century Christians the field of battle is world wide.

The motive of thanksgiving

In order that creation in unison with Christ may sing God's glory through the priestly offering of the Christian people, they must first have conquered creation. This does not refer to the number of things they will have to offer, but to their humanizing of the world; it is the authentic human values that will constitute their offering. In this way as conscientious workmen we shall have anticipated Christ's universal Kingdom.

Is it arbitrary to associate these three motives with the three elements of the Church's mission of holiness—with evangelism, the Eucharist and pastoral care? This mission belongs principally to the priesthood; the laity only participate partially. But its threefold prolongation in time is the specific concern of the laity. It is the same motive with a twofold line of action: the Kingdom of God in and through the history of men, made alive by Jesus Christ.

The reasons for Christian activity in the world are those of opening out human communities to the Gospel, being of service to the brethren and consecrating the world to God. These reasons compel us to reflect on our motives in order to see whether they are genuine or bogus. And we need to use a keen mind on this constantly.

We sometimes get the impression that the only thing that matters to Christians is the idea governing what they do. Armed with good intentions they rush to devote every single thing to Christ. They act as though these things had no value in themselves, but only in so far as they are spiritually annexed and put to pious uses. Label every institution, every product of history with a Christian ticket and straightway it becomes Christ's.

The good intention can be appreciated. A man is a Christian and also engaged in some sector of the world's work. Faith inclines to be totalitarian; the believer finds that it is a new and all-penetrating influence. He wants to make every second Christian and his whole life one in the unity of faith. If he is an economist, it will be as a Christian; similarly if he is a politician; and even when he eats. But it is one thing to unify his life in this way, and quite another to mix a sort of Christian cocktail out of economics and politics, imagining that these and not only his life have become one in Christ.

It is a great temptation, especially as regards politics, to connect it with Christ so that it will be at his service. The aim of politics is to organize technical instruments and social activities for the good of the community which should be friendly, united and just. But the Kingdom of God is also a community of this kind. Christ gathers men in the love of God and of each other. Of course that is for life in eternity, but still it is an extension of human and political roots. If it were not, why should we not draw laws from the Gospel for the political organization of the world? In the past there has been the medieval Christian State in the West, the dream of Christendom. Today men talk of the unity of mankind centring round the pope. These express various attempts to work out politics from the Gospel. But matters are not so simple. The Gospel and the Church contain the laws of the Kingdom of God. The political unity of the world, on the other hand, has to be fashioned from conditions produced by time and history. On these judgement is a result of experience. There is no uniform Christian recipe for political situations. There is only Christian inspiration for political labours.

Here is an example: There is a movement towards European unity as against conflicting national egoisms. It is a step towards the gathering of men together in world peace. Christ certainly would wish believers to forward it. But as regards its technical organization, whether it is to be socialist or federal, faith has little to contribute. The facts, available information and personal experience of affairs can alone be of any use.

For Christian action must begin by respecting the laws that belong to the realities it is concerned to inspire. Christ's reign over human life and civilization is hidden within them. It becomes visible, and the unity of the universe in him becomes manifest only in the world to come. To pretend that it is possible now is an illusion. A Christian brings booty into the Kingdom now only by acting as leaven, by an inner transformation. All other method leads to a mirage and shallow clericalism.

So a Christian owes a twofold loyalty. He must be loyal to Christ and to specifically Christian motives for action. He must be loyal to creation and history which he must bring to Christ. The best intentions cannot dispense with technical competence and informed activity.

Some Christians have the boldness of the takeover bid. Others do nothing at all because they feel themselves unworthy. They want to make sure that every step is authentically Christian and that their own intentions are of unblemished integrity. Such certainty is not frequent in real life.

There is a risk of some alloy in all Christian activity. And it should be scrutinized for this beforehand. But forceful action involves risk. The point is not to be obstinate, and to be willing to alter things at the bidding of experience. Ambiguity always accompanies choice in the practical sphere. Theories may be logically incompatible, but in practice they may work out more harmoniously. Sometimes, of course, duties may conflict and a Christian may be tempted to resign, preferring the impossible total good to that which is partially attainable.

To accept the alloy in all temporal activity without worrying about it is not a sign that conscience is decaying. If one tries for the impossible and does not do what is in one's grasp, it is a sin of omission.

Adult Christianity is the contemporary programme. It has many aspects. Among the most important of them is the fact that an adult Christian is aware that he is both actively engaged in the Church and also has to lead a responsible life in the world with less excuses for deception than non-Christians. "All things are yours, for you are Christ's and Christ is God's."

CHAPTER XII

THE CHURCH OF THE SAINTS

In *Les deux sources de la morale et de la religion*, Bergson questioned the Christian saints about the secret of their life. He was drawn by what seemed to him a unique spiritual achievement. He saw clearly that a saint was quite different from a hero, a superman or a sage. Only the presence of the living God can explain this original outpouring of universal life and love. The power of the Gospel acting in the present can alone account for that spontaneous imitation of Christ and that living illustration of the Sermon on the Mount. Bergson had the good sense to seize the fact of holiness in its essential mystery. And yet had he continued his interrogation of the Christian saints they would have replied: "You have forgotten one vital factor. Our achievement is not merely individual; our experience as Christians is not the result of a solitary relationship with Christ. It is in and through the Church that he has given us a living share in his holiness." This is a fundamental point in Christian life and we will conclude this book by considering it.

THE CHURCH: SEED-BED OF HOLINESS

Primarily the Church is the assembly of those whom God has called to the glory of his Kingdom (1 Thess. 2. 12), the people of God of whom St Peter says: "You are a chosen race, a royal priesthood, a consecrated nation, a people God means to have for himself; it is yours to proclaim the exploits of the God who has called you out of darkness into his marvellous light" (1 Peter 2. 9). A Christian community is a group of human beings who have received the seeds of holiness and who if they grow up will be saints; it is to promote this that it exists. Saints are born from it as from a spiritual womb. Of course it is God who makes them saints, with their free collaboration. But it is within the Christian assembly that God acts and it is there that the believer fulfils his vocation.

The contemporary situation of the Church makes the communal aspect of holiness particularly relevant and important. When Christianity was more embedded in the social structure, secular institutions provided a more reliable backing for the Church's pastoral authority. They took Christian conduct as the norm of social morality and applied it accordingly. The Church had outside support—as much as clericalism could wish for. And the individual Christian benefited from this social support, even though the perils of conformism lay hidden in it.

This Christian social structure has gone; we may regret it, or be glad; in any case it is hopeless to try to halt the Church against the march of time. There has to be an adaptation; we are brought back to the position of Christians before Christendom. The Church has to carry out the commands of the Gospel in the midst of the living community and with its help. Every community contains some members who are weak and sick as well as the strong and fit; good example and the striving towards perfection gives everyone a chance of being true to Christ's law. In our time, when standards of behaviour are everywhere questioned, it is practically impossible for an individual Christian all on his own not to compromise on some point. He has the right to expect from his brethren the help of their prayers, their active friendship, inspiration from their loyalty, criticism when needed and when it genuinely proceeds from love, encouragement to be heroic when special circumstances call for it. Without this neighbourly "building up" a man cannot stand up to the spiritual flabbiness, the moral compromises, the eroticism and professional "fiddling" all around. A worldly ethic claiming to base itself on experience, cunning and realism is always contradicting or hitting at the standards of the Kingdom.

Communal support also has the advantage of presenting its ideas rather than imposing them; freedom is promoted and at the same time the values desired are brought to life.

We may be approaching the time when the Christian community will take itself so seriously that once again those who deliberately resist its will will be thrown out.

> If thy brother does thee wrong, go at once and tax him with it, as a private matter between thee and him; and so, if he will listen to thee, thou hast won thy brother. If he will not listen to thee, take with thee one or two more, that the whole matter may be certified by the voice of two or three witnesses. If he will not listen to thee, then speak of it to the church; and if he will not listen even to the church, then count him all one with the heathen and the publican (Matt. 18. 15–18).

"You too must be built upon him," says St Peter, "stones that live and breathe, into a spiritual fabric; you must be a holy priesthood" (1 Peter 2. 5).

THE CHURCH: SOURCE OF HOLINESS

The Christian community is organized and possesses institutional forms, chief of which are the apostolic hierarchy, the ministry of the word and the sacraments. But the only reason for their existence is holiness, the sole purpose Christ had in mind when he gave his apostles their mission and their responsibility. The institution of the Church is not the setting up of an administration, but an undertaking of holiness. That is why the Church is holy even if priests who carry her responsibility are not; for, in the name of the whole Church they can give what they personally do not possess.

The word of God given for me to inwardly digest is sanctifying. The counsels and directives of Christian authority far from being the commands of a spiritual police force are meant to promote the growth of evangelical holiness, for Christ said: "Keep my commandments."

Above all, the liturgical life of the Church plunges Christians back into the stream that flows from Christ's death and resurrection. At least it does so if sacramental practice is not misunderstood; for the sacraments are not duties externally imposed, something added to the inner movement of grace. Nor are they, as in many religions, rites of religious security to be performed in a given set of circumstances in order to put things right with God. If we keep in mind two essentials we shall not stray from their true meaning. First, Christian grace is communicated by Christ; secondly, Christian grace is shared out in the Church, the seed-bed of holiness. Hence it is that the Church's sacraments are not reducible to individual means of salvation: they are signs, made effective in the world today, of Christ's Alliance with mankind. The Christian participating in the celebration of the sacraments knows that Christ is showing, at that moment, that he is keeping his word and bestowing grace upon the Church; that the Body of Christ is being built up; and that he himself is benefiting from the grace given to this Body.

A normally developing Christian life will therefore be punctuated by contacts with the Lord's person and with the invisible world of the Alliance of which the sacraments are signs. The words: "I am a believer, but I do not practise" may have some theoretical meaning; it is hard to see how they can be justified in the context of a faith whose practical coordinates are the living Christ, the Passover in our time, working in and through the Christian dynamism of which the visible form is the sacramental Church. The saints of all time have grown in Christ by living in the Church with loyalty and integrity. This has not stopped them from working from within for the reform of the Church when the keen sense of her mission to promote holiness has become dim. The saints have always been the only reformers who have succeeded.

THE CHURCH: THE SIGN OF HOLINESS

We are dealing now with the community as well as the institution. The Church, amidst the world, must bear witness to holiness in every one of her aspects. Does our Church resemble, as the Vatican Council hoped it did, a standard raised above the nations, a sign calling to the faith those who have not yet come to believe in Christ? The Gospel proclaimed needs to be authenticated by the Gospel lived, and lived collectively. The divine presence and power of Christ which we proclaim ought to be visible in the collective life of those who affirm that God has intervened. This is particularly necessary in a technical world that mistrusts ideas and raptures and prefers facts. The fact of holiness ought to be the great and abiding miracle at the Church's disposal from the point of view of her missionary presence in the modern world.

The Church will have been really powerful in a period, not when she has enjoyed the fallacious prestige of human acclamation or political or diplomatic triumph, but when the holiness of the Gospel has been her unique concern and when this has borne abundant fruit. The world looks for the coming of saints; they are witnesses of that superhuman destiny which it cannot reach by its own efforts to transcend itself.

THE KINGDOM OF THE SAINTS: THE FUTURE OF THE CHURCH

The Church of eternity is already journeying on the earth. Holiness begins with grace, but it is only fulfilled in glory. Christ was absolutely holy from the moment of his Incarnation, but only at the Resurrection did his humanity attain its total holiness. In the same way, the Church makes her progress towards the glory of the resurrection. So long as she is on earth Christ is continuously withdrawing her from sin in order to lead her to holiness. His sanctifying work will end only with the coming of the holy city from heaven, of which the Apocalypse speaks: "Here is God's tabernacle pitched among men; he will dwell with them, and they will be his own people, and he will be among them, their own God. He will wipe every tear away from their eyes, and there will be no more death, or mourning, or cries of distress, no more sorrow; these old things have passed away" (Apoc. 21. 3–6). So long as she is passing from death to the first resurrection, from the first resurrection to the second, the Church is in the time of hope.

What the Church will be one day, she is already in the person of her Lord, and also in that of Mary who following her Son has bodily entered into glory and is the anticipation of the perfected Church. The saints who have died in the Lord are awaiting the hour of the Kingdom so as to enter bodily into that glory which has already received them in spirit. Mary and the saints, together with Christ and in dependence upon him, are actively concerned with believers who are on the road to holiness; for there is only one Kingdom. That is why we ask the saints to intercede fraternally for us who are still in travail, so that every human life and every moment of history may collaborate in the completion of that purpose which God had formed before the world's creation, that all things shall be gathered together and reconciled in his Kingdom of love and holiness.

We are well assured that everything helps to secure the good of those who love God, those whom he has called in fulfilment of his design. All those who from the first were known to him, he has destined from the first to be moulded into the image of his Son, who is thus to become the eldest born among many brethren. So predestined, he called them; so called, he justified them; so justified, he glorified them (Rom. 8. 28–31).

THE COMMUNITY AND THE INDIVIDUAL IN THE CHURCH

In spite of this, however, it is not rare to meet people whose concern for a faith that is personal entails a kind of mistrust, amounting to a cold war, with respect to the Church. It is not difficult to understand them. If, with Simone Weil, they see the Church as "a gross sociological animal", how can concern for it be serious without degrading that personal relationship to Christ which is faith?

Without going so far as that, we do perhaps sometimes accept the Church as though it were merely a matter of choice, personal faith remaining alongside without being integrated with it. It is a minimal adhesion, without much conviction, to the community, the hierarchical structure and the sacraments. And we are the more inclined to this position if, leaving the faith of a fellow-traveller behind, we have discovered the meaning of a mature faith lived from the Gospel.

Must the Church, then, inevitably sever the personal element in our meeting with Christ? If we think of those believers who bear witness to the fact that they owe the development of their faith to a loyal participation in the Church's life, it would seem not. And yet perhaps there is a need to rediscover that aspect of the Church which echoes the personal call of Christ.

We may recall how the Church began. In the Old Testament the Church was the assembly of Yahweh, made anew by the events of the Passover that freed the people from Egypt. One became a member of that assembly the moment one admitted, by faith in those events, that God was the Liberator. Entry into the Alliance was the condition of faith, and the condition for entry was that of belonging to the assembly of Yahweh which is the Church.

In the New Testament, the Church, of which the assembly in the desert was only the prefigurement, gathered together the believers in the new Passover at Pentecost. The word

Church—a number of people assembled by a personal summons—takes on its full meaning. The people summoned by the Holy Spirit and the apostolic testimony accept the Easter message through faith and baptism and become the people of the new Alliance. Not for a second did it enter their heads that there could be belief in Christ which did not at once entail a definite entry into the Christian community.

How is it then that some Christians feel estranged by the community as though it threatened to make their personal faith lazy and gregarious? It may be that they were born in the Church but have never come into it with conscious faith seeking communion with others who have been freed by the Gospel.

A man who has come into the Church with a believing "Amen" to the personal summons of Christ comes into a fellowship of believers. Intelligent relationship begins. The general faith in no way dispenses the individual from maturing his own conviction in the faith. Nor does it exercise irrational pressure, but it promotes integrity and courage and gives daily help to each in his personal calling.

An assembly of believing and free men communicating in the Holy Spirit who dwells in each of them and unites them all together—such is the Church. What a force it ought to be against idolatry, religious fellow-travelling and every form of slackness!

But the Church does not exist simply as a community of believers and brothers. It exists also as an institution, an authority, a sacrament. Some will feel that this intensifies the threat of depersonalization, adding the weight of things put apart as sacred, external customs and obligations, administration, the whole social set-up.

It cannot, in fact, be denied that the Christian institution has practised and still practises, when it is abused, a form of power politics and that in doing so it may estrange the believer. But if we go back in faith to the will of its founder, Christ, and to him who promulgated it, the Spirit of Pentecost, we find nothing of the kind. The institution is at the service of the Alliance sealed at Easter: it is God's Word for mankind; it is a sign of grace for the community and its members; it is an expression of the communion of saints and brings that communion about.

If we consider the sacraments, we find that they are not ritual measures of security, parts of a kind of electric-shock religion, but a personal activity of Christ meeting the free purpose of his believers. They awaken faith; they demand a pure heart; they stimulate personal relations.

If we consider apostolic authority, we find that unlike worldly authority it does not demand conformism and discipline. It is the service, in the name of the Lord Jesus, of those entrusted to its care, in the spirit of the advice of St Peter: "Be shepherds to the flock God has given you. Carry out your charge as God would have it done, cordially, not like drudges, generously, not in the hope of sordid gain; not tyrannizing, each in his own sphere, but setting an example, as best you may, to the flock" (1 Peter 5. 2–4).

Thus all things in the Church as an institution express relationships of personal grace and charity. No anonymity, no soulless machinery, no faceless bureaucracy. Should this not always be the case, it is a sign that we have to fight for the purity of the spirit of Jesus as shown in the Church of Pentecost. It is not an indication that we should quit.

To enter into the community of believers, to see that one must obey the institution, is at the same time to be at one with the influence which the Church exercises in the world. History, unhappily, provides ready arguments against this statement. In such things as the Inquisition, the holy war, the "spiritual conquest" of the barbarians, the wars of religion, the Christian apostolate has been stained by violence. What we read in the Acts of the Apostles about the upsurge of hope at the beginning of the Christian movement enables us to pass a severe judgement on these later deviations. The Gospel must be carried to the ends of the earth, for it is for all nations and all flesh shall see the salvation of God. Christ will not repeat his earthly career and there will not be two Easters or two Pentecosts. The Church cannot refrain from her public testimony: she cannot be silenced. But her testimony must be gentle and respectful of men. It must allow every man to face it with his conscience and to come forward as a person to inquire who Christ is.

Nothing is more personal than the publicity of the Gospel. It seeks to reach human freedom in the vast network of human consciousness by the influence of the personal word of God. Nothing should be more repugnant to the Church of Christ than mass suggestion or clandestine persuasion or psychological trickery—forms of power all of them in opposition to the Gospel from which the Church originated. But here also it is extremely difficult for the Church to be what she ought to be and no other. It is a matter which concerns us all.

Persons in the Church: That is the Holy Spirit's programme of action, and it will always succeed in spite of the sinful tendencies that work against it.

"Our Church is the Church of the saints," wrote Bernanos. "To become a saint, what bishop would not give up his ring, his mitre and crozier, what cardinal his purple, what pope his white cassock, his camerlengos, his Swiss guard and all his temporalities? ... The whole of this great display of wisdom, discipline, magnificence and majesty is nothing in itself, unless charity gives it life. Mediocrity of course only wants from it a sound insurance against the risks of the divine anger. That does not matter. The youngest child in Sunday School knows that the blessing of all churchmen given together would bring peace only to those souls ready to receive it, to men of good will. No rite has the power to dispense from loving. Our Church is the Church of the saints."

SELECT BIBLIOGRAPHY

In this series: DAUJAT, Jean: *The Theology of Grace*; BARS, Henry: *Faith, Hope and Charity*; PONTIFEX, Mark: *Providence and Freedom* (American edn, *Freedom and Providence*).

AQUINAS, St Thomas: *Summa Theologica*, 3 volumes, translated by Fathers of the English Dominican Province, London, Burns and Oates, and New York, Benziger, 1948.

BRUNO DE JÉSUS-MARIE, O.C.D. (Editor): *Love and Violence*, London and New York, Sheed and Ward, 1954.

DANIÉLOU, Jean, S.J.: *The Christian Today*, New York, Desclée, 1960.

FARRELL, Walter, O.P.: *A Companion to the Summa*, Volume I, London and New York, Sheed and Ward, 1941.

GILLMAN, Gerard, S.J.: *The Primacy of Charity in Moral Theology*, London, Burns and Oates, and Westminster, Md, Newman Press, 1960.

LEBRETON, Jules, S.J.: *The Life and Teaching of Jesus Christ*, London, Burns and Oates, and New York, Macmillan, 1958.

SCHEEBEN, Matthias J.: *Mysteries of Christianity*, St Louis, Herder, 1946.

SHEED, F. J.: *Theology and Sanity*, London and New York, Sheed and Ward, 1947.

SMITH, G. D. (Editor): *The Teaching of the Catholic Church*, London, Burns and Oates, and New York, Macmillan, 1947

WATKIN, Aelred, O.S.B.: *The Enemies of Love*, London, Burns and Oates, and New York, Kenedy, 1958.

2007